THE BELIEF IN PROGRESS

THE
BELIEF IN PROGRESS

By

JOHN BAILLIE

D.Litt., D.D., LL.D.

Professor of Divinity in the University of Edinburgh
Chaplain to the King in Scotland

'For they that say such things declare
plainly that they seek a country'

CHARLES SCRIBNER'S SONS, NEW YORK

1951

PREFACE

In the hope that it may prove of interest to a wider circle, I here offer the somewhat compressed substance of a course of lectures delivered in the Post-Graduate School of Theology in the University of Edinburgh, during the winter of 1946-7 and repeated two years later. The lectures contained ampler quotation from source materials, especially of the seventeenth and eighteenth centuries, than I have been able to retain in the book, but I have allowed much of the quotation from present-day writers to stand.

I am most grateful to my brother, Professor Donald Baillie of St. Andrews, for having read the book in typescript, and to Professor J. Y. Campbell of Westminster College, Cambridge, and Professor J. H. S. Burleigh of this University for their careful revision of the proofs. The comments of all three were such as to save me from numerous infelicities and not a few errors.

No doubt errors remain. I have done my best to get things straight, but cannot hope that I have entirely succeeded. My effort will, however, have served some purpose if it encourages the reader to find out for himself where I have gone wrong.

JOHN BAILLIE

Edinburgh
December 1949

ACKNOWLEDGEMENTS

THANKS are due to the respective publishers and others for permission to reproduce extracts from the following copyright works:
Messrs. Allen and Unwin for passages by the late Edwyn Bevan, Dr. C. H. Dodd, and Professor P. Tillich from *The Kingdom of God and History* (Church, Community and State Series, Vol. III) and from Edwyn Bevan's *Hellenism and Christianity*; the Cambridge University Press for passages from Professor A. N. Whitehead's *Process and Reality*; the Clarendon Press for passages from the late R. G. Collingwood's *The Idea of History*, and from the Collected Essays of F. H. Bradley; Messrs. Victor Gollancz for a passage from Professor S. Hook's translation of a letter of F. Engels; Messrs. James Nisbet & Co. for passages from Dr. C. H. Dodd's *History and the Gospel*, Professor Reinhold Niebuhr's *The Nature and Destiny of Man*, and the late Professor O. C. Quick's *The Gospel of the New World*; Penguin Books for passages from Professor V. Gordon Childe's *What Happened in History* and Professor A. D. Ritchie's *Civilization, Science and Religion*; Messrs. C. A. Watts & Co. for passages from Professor Childe's *Man Makes Himself* and *Progress and Archaeology*; and the executors of the late Dr. John Clarke for passages from his *Physical Science in the Time of Nero*.

CONTENTS

CONTENTS

CHAPTER I

PROGRESS AS EMPIRICALLY OBSERVED

§ 1

HISTORIANS agree in regarding belief in progress as one of the ruling ideas in the Western thought of the last hundred and fifty or two hundred years. They agree also in denying to it a similar part in the thought of earlier epochs and other cultures, but when we ask whether it there played any part at all, we receive a somewhat less unanimous answer. Observers of our contemporary situation further agree that the hold of this belief upon the Western mind has of late years seriously weakened, but since their own minds are part of the Western mind, they are naturally much divided as to whether this change gives reason for dismay or for rejoicing. In other words, they differ widely as to whether the belief provides a sound clue to the interpretation of the past and a safe guide to our outlook on the future; both as to whether there has been progress in history, and if so of what kind, and as to whether we have the right to hope for progress in time to come, and if so of what kind. Yet few things can be more important in the present crisis of our Western fortunes than to have a clear mind on these questions.

§ 2

The word 'progress' may be used to connote a continued movement or series of changes in any given direction, as when we speak of our progress on a journey, of the progress of a disease or even, with Hogarth, of the Rake's Progress; but we shall here be concerned only with its more specific meaning as a movement in a direction deemed desirable, a continued change for the better. That some such progress ought to or normally does manifest itself in the life of the individual between the cradle and the grave has always and everywhere been taken for granted. As the child grows to manhood, and the man to riper years, advance is expected, not only at first in strength and stature, but also in the acquisition of various skills, in intelligence, in wisdom and in the settled practice of virtue. Yet whereas increase of intelligence and skill has been thought of as coming by continuous and slow gradation, the case has been different with regard to wisdom and virtue; for no traditional culture has lacked the idea of a crisis of initiation, not to say conversion, which had the effect of more or less abruptly raising the initiate to a new level of insight and attainment in this spiritual sphere. A discrimination has thus been made between the natural progress of the individual as he grows to maturity, and that growth in grace which cannot begin until initiation has taken place. This distinction of nature and grace is, of course, a Christian one, having been formulated in the early Patristic period of Christian thought, but in all ancient cultures there is a feeling after some distinction of this kind.

The progress with which we shall here be concerned is not, however, the progress of the individual during his

brief span of life, but the progress of the race from generation to generation. This is the idea which has been so
characteristic of the modern European mind, and of whose
presence in earlier periods and other traditions the historians speak so doubtfully. It is true that during the
period when this idea was most dominant among us, it
exercised a certain reflex action upon our conception of
the progress of the individual. That, like the other, now
tended to be thought of only in terms of slow but steady
gradation. Either the distinction between natural progress and progress in grace faded out or, where it was
conserved, a much more confident view was assumed of
the progress in grace which individuals actually made this
side the grave—men all the time rising on stepping-stones
of their dead selves to higher things. This, however, is a
side-issue; and since in one form or another the idea of
individual progress has always and everywhere been present in the human mind, the main question now confront-
ing us may well be stated as follows: Does history reveal,
and have we any ground for expecting it to reveal, a
pattern of advance which reproduces *in magno* the pattern
manifested or expected *in parvo* in the biographies of
individuals? May we legitimately, in Pascal's phrase, regard 'the whole sequence of human beings, throughout
the whole course of the ages, as the same man living on
and learning something all the time'?[1]

---

[1] *Fragment d'un Traité du Vide;* see Brunschvicg, *Blaise Pascal: Opuscules et
Pensées* (1897), p. 80.

§ 3

However, the best preliminary to the inquiry whether or not there is progress in history is to inquire into the history of the idea that there is. The two inquiries are in themselves quite distinct. The history of progress is a different tale from the history of belief in it. It is possible that men have progressed without knowing it, or again that they believed they were progressing when in fact they were not. Yet the two histories may have influenced one another. The observation of actual progress may have been a cause of belief in it, while again belief in the thing may have aided the thing itself. If progress is possible, and if it be something that comes to those who seek it, its realization will depend upon belief in its possibility, and disbelief will work against it. For this reason we shall not be able to keep the two histories entirely separate in our exposition.

Our starting-point, however, must be with the history of the belief. It may be said with a fair degree of confidence that the idea of progress from generation to generation is entirely absent from the mind of the ruder cultures. There is here no sense of history, no historical memory, no awareness that things ever had been or ever would be substantially different from their present familiar condition. Each tribe has its own traditions which it faithfully observes, but it has no idea how these came into being nor even any thought of raising the question, nor again does it ever contemplate the possibility of any innovation being made on them.

But the higher and more reflective civilizations of the ancient world present a different picture. These have all some sense of their own past, and a more or less definite view concerning the origin of their existing tradition. They know that things have not always been as they are now, that men have not always possessed the knowledge and skill now at their command. The account they give of the origin of this knowledge and skill is in part mythological, in part legendary, and in some part also genuinely historical. Among the Hebrews, for example, the realization that their present condition represented an advance upon the days of long ago is reflected in their stories of Abel as the first herdsman, of Cain as the first planter of crops, of Tubal as the first smith, and of Jubal as the first instrumental musician. Among the Greeks we have the mythical figures of Prometheus who stole the first fire from the hearth of Zeus, and of Hephaestus the skilful artificer. There is, however, a genuine element of historical memory in the accounts given of the origin of the national traditions as embodied in law and custom. In the thought both of the Hebrews and of the Greeks the figures of the great lawgivers played an especially prominent part. Both peoples tended towards the exclusive association of the origin of their laws with the figures of individual wise men, the Hebrews with the figure of Moses, the Greek city-states with those of Minos, Zaleucus, Lycurgus, Draco and Solon, where modern historians would speak rather of a slow process of quiet accretion to which these lawgivers gave definitive form. But in any case there is here an evident awareness that the treasures

5

of wisdom now available had not always been at men's command.

§ 4

In this, however, there is nothing that yet deserves the name of belief in progress. There is no thought of a continuing process either in the past or into the future, but only an account of the abrupt origin in the comparatively remote past of a present condition now conceived as blessedly static. It is only among the Greeks, and those influenced by them, that a further stage was ever reached, while even in Greece it did not emerge until the fifth century B.C.—and then only among a few of the more reflective thinkers. In that century we find the poet-philosopher Xenophanes writing that:

οὔτοι ἀπ᾽ ἀρχῆς πάντα θεοὶ θνητοῖσ᾽ ὑπέδειξαν,
ἀλλὰ χρόνῳ ζητοῦντες ἐφευρίσκουσιν ἄμεινον.

'The gods did not reveal everything to men from the beginning, but by searching men find out in time what is best.'[1]

It is to the historians of the period that we should naturally look for the expansion of this statement, yet for the most part we shall look in vain. The Greek historians, like their Roman successors, had no large outlook upon the fortunes of humanity in general, being for the most part mere chroniclers of some recent chapter of events in their own homeland. As the late Professor Collingwood expressed it, the ancient Greek historian 'was only the autobiographer of his generation'.[2]

[1] Diels, *Fragmente der Vorsokratiker*, Xenophanes, Fragment 18.
[2] *The Idea of History* (1946), p. 27.

The most we can point to is therefore the well-known first chapter of Thucydides in which he prefaces his account of the war between Athens and Sparta with some remarks about the earlier course of events in Greece. He too is writing no more than a chronicle of his own times, of a war that is going on as he writes. But he is anxious to exhibit it as the greatest war of all time, and to show that earlier wars had been fought between much weaker and less settled states, with much smaller forces and much less efficient armaments. In order to establish this he must say something about earlier periods. He is, however, very sceptical about the trustworthiness of the available information concerning the events, not merely of the remote past, but even of the immediately preceding age; 'for men accept from one another without discrimination (ἀβασανίστως, "without applying a touchstone") reports of what happened in the past.' Therefore 'we must be careful not to believe either what the poets have sung concerning them, making them greater by their embellishments, or what the chroniclers have put together in a way more pleasant to the hearing than truthful, accounts which cannot be tested and most of which have become untrustworthy and mythoid (μυθώδης, "of the nature of a tale") through the lapse of time'.

However, making the best of such evidence as is available Thucydides concludes that former ages in Greece 'were not great in wars or in anything else'. The country now called Hellas had formerly no settled population. Being prevented by fear of each other's depredations, the tribes did not cultivate the land beyond what was barely necessary to satisfy their immediate needs, they did not accumulate wealth or build large cities, and they were migratory in their habits. This 'weakness of the ancients' is seen also in the fact that until the Trojan war the tribes were never united in any common action. There was no safe and settled commerce between them, but only piracy at sea and landward plunder of each other's towns which were 'unwalled and built like villages'. Even in his account of the Trojan war Homer, though he has various ways of designating the combined armies—as Danāans, Argives, Achaeans—never uses the collective term Hellenes for them, and never speaks of 'the barbarians', because this distinction had not yet been made. Moreover, Thucydides proceeds, the total forces engaged in that war were not large. In the age that followed conditions in Greece were still unsettled, 'so that it could not grow peacefully'. Finally, however, the city-states became wealthier and more powerful, though it was but very recently that the number and size of the naval vessels had reached anything like the present standard. There were, however, 'different impediments to the growth of the different states'; there was the menace of Persia, and there was the fact that most of the states were ruled by tyrants who, thinking only of the safety and aggrandizement of their own persons and families, 'did nothing worth mentioning' except in wars with their immediate neighbours, and prevented Greece for a long time both from any noteworthy common enterprise and from bolder action on the part of individual states. Meanwhile, however, the Lacedemonians had enjoyed good laws, and they had never been ruled by tyrants; they now deposed the tyrants in the rest of Greece and later joined in confederacy with the Athenians to defeat the Medes. Soon these two confederate powers quarrelled, dividing between them the loyalties of the other Greek states. They are now the leading powers in Hellas, one at sea, the other on the land; and the power of each is greater than was formerly the combined power of the two. Hence the Peloponnesian war, which Thucydides begins to chronicle almost as soon as it has started, is the greatest of all wars, more fraught with destiny than any war had ever been.

So runs Thucydides's argument.[1] Its importance for our present enquiry is that it represents the most enlightened view yet put forward by anybody about the earlier course of human history. It reveals its author as a man who clearly knew that the period of civilization in which he himself was living, and which formed the proximate past of his native land, had behind it an indefinitely long period of such barbaric conditions as he knew still to exist in regions not far to the north.

§ 5

That is about as far as the ancient historians carry us, but the ancient philosophers, though less empirical in their approach, carry us a little farther. The two great philosophical systems of the post-Aristotelian period were of such a kind as to demand for their completeness some account of the origin of mankind and the growth of

[1] *De Bello Peloponnesiaco*, i, 1-21.

human civilization. It is, therefore, to the Stoic and Epicurean writings, but particularly to the latter, that we must look for further light.

The extant fragments of Epicurus's own writings contain only one passage which bears upon the subject of the growth of civilization. We must take it for granted, he writes, that human nature was taught and constrained to do all kinds of things by circumstances themselves, but that later on reason improved on what had thus been suggested by nature and made further discoveries, in some periods very rapidly, in others more slowly. The single example he gives concerns language, which he believes to have originated from natural sounds produced by reflex action, but to have been afterwards deliberately developed by different nations in order to make their meaning clearer and less ambiguous.[1]

But it is in Latin literature, in the great poem of Lucretius, that we find what is at the same time the fullest development of the Epicurean teaching, and by far the fullest account which the ancient world has to offer us of the growth of human culture. How far Lucretius was dependent for the details of his account on writings of Epicurus which are now lost to us, it is no doubt impossible to say.

In the fifth book of his poem[2] Lucretius presents us with a vivid picture of our earliest ancestors as a hardy race, living on nuts and berries, wearing no clothes, dwelling in forests and caves, 'having no regard for the com-

[1] Epicurus, *The Extant Remains*, ed. Cyril Bailey (1926), pp. 44-6.
[2] *De rerum natura*, v, 925-1457.

mon good and knowing not the use of any customs or laws'—so that, for example, their sexual intercourse was entirely promiscuous. Then, when they got them huts and skins, learned the use of fire, and became monogamous, 'the human race began to grow soft'. They formed friendships with one another, each agreeing not to attack the other but to join in the protection of the women and children; 'with cries and gestures signifying in broken words that it is right for all to pity the weak.' The origin of language is then described at length, and the origin of the employment of fire for cooking and heating. Next, men of outstanding ability gradually showed their fellows 'how to change their former life for new ways'. Kings began to build cities, to accumulate and apportion wealth, until their greed and ambition led them to fight one another in bloody wars, and things were brought 'to the utmost dregs of confusion'. At the same time religious ideas began to gain sway over men's minds, and religious observances over their lives. Then followed the discovery of the use of metals, there being first a copper and bronze age, and then an iron age.

'The ancient weapons were hands and finger-nails and teeth, stones and branches torn from trees, and flames and fire when these became known. Afterwards was discovered the strength of iron and bronze; but the use of bronze was learned before that of iron, it being both more malleable and more plentiful. . . . Then by small degrees (*minutatim*) the iron sword gained ascendancy, the bronze sickle becoming a thing of scorn.'[1]

After iron came woven cloth (*textile post ferrum*); then

[1] Ibid., 1283–94.

the arts of sowing seed, grafting and tilling. Forts were built and ships constructed. And then at last poets began to celebrate mighty deeds in song.

'Nor had letters been invented much before this, and that is why our age cannot look back to see former events, unless reason is able to point to some remaining traces. Ships and agriculture, fortifications, laws, weapons, roads, clothing and everything of that sort, each and all the prizes and luxuries of life, songs and pictures and the polishing of shapely statues—all these did the experience of the active mind teach little by little to men who progressed step by step (*paulatim docuit pedetentim progredientes*). So little by little the passage of time brings one thing after another into our view, and reason lifts it into the circle of light. For by the arts of their mind they saw one thing after another grow clear, until they reached the highest point.'[1]

So does Lucretius conclude his remarkable account. Much interest has naturally been aroused by the fact that the very word 'progress' is here introduced. Nevertheless this is not the whole of the story. Lucretius is far from regarding this 'progress' as an unmixed blessing, or most of the changes involved in it as being changes for the better. He has offered what he regards as a faithful account of what probably happened, but he himself follows his master Epicurus in manywise preferring the simple 'life according to nature'. Savage man, he says, was 'hard', whereas the advance of civilization made him 'grow soft'.

'Then it was want of food that gave over their fainting frames to death, now it is surfeit that destroys them.'[2]

'Afterwards property was invented and gold was found, which soon robbed of honour both the strong and the comely; since, however strong men are, and however comely in body, they usually

[1] Ibid., 1445-57.　　　　[2] Ibid., 1007-8.

follow the rich. Yet if a man's life were governed by true reason, it were great riches for him to live on a little with contented mind —for a little is always available.'[1]

In his nostalgic idealization of the happy savage he rivals the romantics of our late eighteenth century:

'Often stretched in groups on the soft grass beside running water under the boughs of some tall tree, they would at small cost delight their bodies, especially when the weather smiled and the season of the year painted the grass with flowers. Then were wont to be jests and talk and peals of sweet laughter. For then was the rustic muse in its prime. . . . The wakeful also found solace for lost sleep in guiding their voices through many notes, in following a tune, and letting their curved lips wander over the reed-pipes. Whence even to-day watchmen preserve these traditions, and have lately learned to keep proper tune, though they get no whit more enjoyment out of it than did the woodland race of the earthborn. For what we have gives supreme delight and is reckoned the best, unless we have already known something more pleasant; but when later we find something better, it spoils and changes our taste for everything old. . . . Then it was skins, but now it is gold and purple to vex men's life with care and wear it out with war; and in this it is surely we who are more at fault. For without the skins the naked earthborn men would have been tortured with cold, whereas it does not harm us in the least to be without a purple robe worked with gold and great figures, so long as only we have a plain man's coat to cover us. Thus does mankind ever labour vainly and to no purpose, consuming his life with empty cares, and for no other reason than that he does not understand the limits of possession or up to what point true pleasure can ever be increased. And this has by small degrees (*minutatim*) carried life out into the deep, and from the bottom of the deep has stirred up the mighty billows of war.'[2]

At the beginning of his sixth book Lucretius follows

[1] Ibid., 1113–19.   [2] Ibid., 1392–1435.

this up by claiming that the way of true wisdom had at last been discovered by Epicurus.

'For when he saw that mortals had now ready to hand nearly everything they needed for living, and that life was as safely established as it could well be; when he saw how men abounded in wealth and honour and renown, swelling with pride in the good repute of their children—while for all that not one of them sat at home with a less anxious heart; saw also how without ceasing they tormented themselves in their own despite, and were constrained to rage with savage complainings; then he understood that the flaw was in the vessel itself, and that this flaw tainted with corruption all that came into the vessel from without. . . . And so with truth-telling words he cleansed men's hearts, set a limit to fear and to desire, showed us what is that highest good towards which we all strive, and pointed out the way to it—the narrow track by which alone we may reach it in a straight course.'[1]

Part of this way was a return to 'the life according to nature', but another part was the expulsion from our minds of those religious ideas which, as we have seen, had developed with developing civilization.

Furthermore it must be remembered that already in his second book Lucretius had argued, in accordance with the view then generally received, that the period of the world's growth must be followed by a period of decline and ultimate disintegration. There comes a time when all bodies, including our own world,

'touch the highest pinnacle of their growth, and after that by small degrees age breaks their strength and mature vigour and dissolves them into what is worse. . . . So therefore even the walls of the wide world will be stormed all round, and will lapse into crumbling ruin. Indeed even now its life is broken, and the worn-out earth, which

[1] vi, 9–28.

once produced all the species and brought to birth the huge bodies of wild beasts, scarce brings forth tiny animals. . . . Moreover of her own accord she first created for mortals the bright crops and happy pasture-lands, which now scarce wax great even when increased by our toil. . . . And now the aged ploughman shakes his head and sighs ever and again that the labour of his hands has come to nought; and when he compares the present with the past he often praises the fortunes of his fathers, and grumbles how the race of the ancients, full of piety, easily supported life on narrow plots of ground, since formerly each man had a much smaller portion of land than he has now. Also the dresser of the worn-out, shrivelled vine wearies heaven in railing gloomily at the trend of the times, not comprehending that all things decay little by little and go to the tomb worn out by age and length of days.'[1]

Yet when, early in the fifth book, Lucretius is arguing against the idea that our world had no beginning but was from everlasting, he lets himself be carried away into saying that it is probably still in its first youth.

'Indeed, as I believe, the whole world is in its youth, and the nature of the world of recent date, and had its beginning not long ago. Wherefore even now some arts are being perfected and some are in process of growing; improvements are still being made in ships, and only lately did musicians discover tuneful melodies. Finally, the nature and reason of things has but lately been discovered, and I am the first to turn it into the speech of my native land.'[2]

Lucretius's understanding of the development of civilization, slowly and by small gradations, from an early savagery is indeed a notable achievement. It cannot fail to remind us of the accounts of the early progress of the race which we have, since the beginning of the nineteenth century, been accustomed to receive from our modern

[1] ii, 1130–1174.   [2] v, 330–7.

archaeologists and palaeanthropologists. Nor is the resemblance by any means accidental. Modern archaeology has been largely positivist in its inspiration. It has consciously stood aside from the traditional theological accounts of human origins, attempting to read the facts by way of empirical evidence based on what Lucretius calls *vestigia*. It has not always directly challenged the theological accounts, being frequently ready to allow that they too might enclose an aspect of the truth. But very often it has directly challenged them in the interest of a naturalistic outlook on life and the world. And this is the interest that moves Lucretius. The single concern of his poem is to show that the theological account of the origin of the universe and of everything in it, including man, is without foundation, and that the contrary account given by the Greek atomists, and above all by Epicurus, is the whole and only truth. Reality consists of nothing, he believes, but falling atoms, and every real thing is but a chance collocation of such atoms. Man was not created by God but was 'earthborn'. There was no Golden Age at the beginning of his history such as other Greeks and Romans liked to imagine, nor any fall from such an age to our present estate. Rather has there been a rise than a fall, and it is of that rise that Lucretius offers so impressive an account. But his interest in the rise goes no further than this. It has at last brought forth *one* good thing, namely, the wisdom of Epicurus. Most of the other things it has brought forth are doubtful blessings. Lucretius's philosophy of history is thus as far as possible from being an optimistic one. The most he hopes from the future is that a greater number of men may attain the inward tranquillity which comes from facing squarely the dismal truth concerning the nature of things which was discovered (and first squarely faced) by Epicurus.

Passing from Epicurean to Stoic, we may profitably compare these views of Lucretius with some well-known remarks made on the subject of progress by Seneca in his *Physical Researches* more than a century later and within the lifetime of St. Paul. The godless naturalism of the Epicureans was repugnant to the Stoics, but both philosophies equally excluded any general optimism regarding the course of history and prevented their adherents from taking delight in the advance of knowledge except so far as it aided them in resigning themselves to things as they are—as Zeno no less than Epicurus had resigned himself. That there is such a thing as the progress of knowledge Seneca well understands; he knows it has had place in the past, and he believes it will be continued in the future. Yet he is only led to speak of it incidentally, in order to excuse his ignorance of the nature of comets. Why should we be surprised at such ignorance, he asks, seeing that it is not yet many hundred years since the Greeks began to understand the movements of the stars?

'And there are many nations at the present hour who merely know the face of the sky and do not yet understand why the moon is obscured in an eclipse. It is but recently indeed that science brought home to ourselves assured knowledge on the subject. The day will yet come when the progress of research through long ages will reveal to sight the mysteries of nature that are now concealed. ... The day will yet come when posterity will be amazed that we remained ignorant of things that will to them seem so plain.'

'Let us not be surprised that what is buried so deeply should be unearthed so slowly.'

'Many discoveries are reserved for the ages still to be, when our memory shall have perished. The world is a poor affair if it do not contain matter for investigation for the whole world in every age.'[1]

In a modern setting some of these phrases would imply an optimistic outlook on the future. But Seneca is no optimist. The advance of knowledge, he tells us, would be slow enough, even if we bestowed all our efforts on it, but actually, so far as he could see, the men of his own time were bestowing all their efforts on the discovery of new vices.

'Do you wonder that wisdom has not yet attained her perfect work? Why, vice has not yet wholly revealed herself. It is still in its infancy, and yet on it we bestow all our efforts; our eyes and our hands are its slaves. Who attends the school of wisdom now? . . . Philosophy gets never a thought. And so it comes to pass that, far from advance being made toward the discovery of what the older generations left insufficiently investigated, many of their discoveries are being lost.'[2]

Furthermore, Seneca is quite sure that the earth is heading for a final physical catastrophe, which will at the same time mark the end of the present cosmic cycle with the complete obliteration of all its achievements and the beginning of the next. This catastrophe will come by deluge or by conflagration or by both.

'Both will take place when God has seen fit to end the old order, and bring in a better. Fire and water are lords of the earth. From

---

[1] *Quaestiones naturales*, vii. 25, 30, 31. In these and the following passages I have availed myself of the excellent translation of John Clarke entitled *Physical Science in the Time of Nero* (1910).
[2] Op. cit., vii. 32.

these it took its rise, and in these it will find its grave. So when a new creation of the world has been resolved on by Heaven, the sea will be let loose on us from above; or it may be the raging fire, if another variety of destruction is Heaven's will. . . . Therefore, there will one day come an end to all human life and interests. The elements of the earth must all be dissolved or utterly destroyed in order that they all may be created anew in innocence, and that no remnant may be left to tutor men in vice. . . . A single day will see the burial of all mankind. All that the long forbearance of fortune has produced, all that has been reared to eminence, all that is famous and all that is beautiful, great thrones, great nations—all will descend into the one abyss, will be overthrown in one hour. . . . When the destruction of the human race is consummated . . . the ancient order of things will be recalled. Every living creature will be created afresh. The earth will receive a new man ignorant of sin, born under happier stars. But they, too, will retain their innocence only while they are new. Vice quickly creeps in. . . .'[1]

§ 6

What we have here is a general understanding of the possibilities of progress in knowledge set in the context of a profoundly pessimistic outlook on history. As we turn our attention from classical literature to the writings of the early Fathers of the Christian Church, we find a situation that at first looks very much the same. It was now generally understood that physical knowledge and skill had advanced in the past, and that they would be likely to advance further in the future; and this understanding was inherited by the Christian from the pagan thinkers; but as little by the one as by the other was it made the

[1] Op. cit., iii. 28, 29, 30.

basis of any general optimism. This may be illustrated by means of the following passage from St. Augustine's *City of God*, written in the first quarter of the fifth century.

'In addition to the arts of living well and of attaining to immortal felicity, arts which are called virtues and which are given to the children of the promise and of the Kingdom only by the grace of God which is in Christ, have not so many and so great arts been invented and applied by human genius, partly of necessity and partly of free will, that this admirable mental and rational ability, as shown even in the quest of dangerous and pernicious as well as of merely superfluous things, bears witness to the remarkable quality of that nature which can invent, learn and apply such things? What wonderful, what stupendous results human industry has reached in clothing and housing! How it has advanced in agriculture and navigation! With what variety of invention it has thought out the designs of vases, statues and pictures, and with what skill executed these! What wonderful spectacles are exhibited in the theatres, incredible to those who only hear report of them! How many ways have been found of catching, killing and taming wild animals! For the destruction of men themselves how many kinds of poisons, weapons and mechanical contrivances have been discovered, and how many medicaments and appliances for the preservation and restoration of their health! What condiments have been found to stimulate the appetite and please the palate! And what a multitude and variety of signs there are to express and communicate our thoughts, with speech and writing as the chief among them! What graces of rhetoric there are to delight the mind! What a wealth and diversity of songs to soothe the ear! What musical instruments and styles of harmony have been devised! What expertness has been reached in measures and numbers and in tracing the orderly movements of the stars! None can exhaust the tale of what thought has thus discovered, especially if instead of such a general view details were to be mentioned. Finally, who can do justice even to the genius shown by philosophers and heretics in the defence of errors and falsities? For what we are speaking of at the moment is the nature of the human mind by which this mortal life is adorned, and not of the faith and way of truth by which immortal life is attained.'[1]

St. Augustine thus understands not a little of the triumphs of human achievement in respect of knowledge, inventiveness and craftsmanship. He recognizes that these may be used for the adornment of life, but he believes them more often misused for its abasement. They are in themselves ambivalent, as capable of wrong as of right application. Nor does he esteem too highly the kind of adornment they provide, since it has little to do with the attainment of that true and everlasting felicity on which alone his inmost heart is set. His chief interest in the recital of these triumphs is to show with what wonderful powers the human race has been endowed by God, and how greatly these powers must have been corrupted from the first man downwards, seeing in what wickedness and misery the race is now sunk.

Lucretius, Seneca, St. Augustine—Epicurean, Stoic and Christian—all took what moderns would regard as a pessimistic view of the general course of our mortal life, yet each had his own solace, finding something good to which his soul might cleave. The Epicurean found it in that very renunciation of hope which springs from the frank acceptance of a naturalist philosophy, and in the consequent freedom from desire and contentment with a simple life. The Stoic found it in that differently adjusted renunciation of hope and freedom from desire that spring from passive acceptance of all actual events as divinely ordained. But

[1] *De civitate dei*, xxii. 24.

the Christian found it in the emergence of a new kind of hope—of which more anon.

The view of history represented by St. Augustine was destined to dominate the thought of Western culture for a thousand years. Is there anywhere to be found in the literature of this long period a statement concerning the progress of human knowledge and invention that materially goes beyond that passage from *The City of God*? It is difficult to know where to look for such.

§ 7

Thanks, however, to the immense labours of explorers, archaeologists, historians and geographers during the modern period, and especially during the last century and a half, we to-day know a thousand times more about the gradual growth of human knowledge and discovery than did Lucretius, Seneca and St. Augustine. We have, of course, the advantage of knowing the story of the further development between their day and ours; but we are also able to trace the story backward from their day with far greater confidence, with far greater precision, and in far greater detail than these were able to do. Our modern pre-historians confirm Lucretius's distinction of the stone from the bronze-copper ages, and these again from the iron age. They do so on the strength of excavated remains of older cultures, yet here we are presented with something of a problem, since Lucretius knew very little of such *vestigia* and gives the impression of having reached his conclusions as much by deduction from his philosophical principles as from strictly empirical evidence. But our pre-historians now make much nicer distinctions within these ages, telling us successively of the old stone age, the middle stone age, the new stone age, the copper age, the early and late bronze ages and the iron age, and then further sub-dividing many of these into successive periods. Convenient summaries of the story will be found in the popular works of Professor V. Gordon Childe, himself a distinguished spade-worker in the field—*Man Makes Himself* (1936), *What Happened in History* (1942) and *Progress and Archaeology* (1944); or in Mr. Christopher Dawson's erudite and admirably written though less first-hand *Age of the Gods* (1928). Mr. Dawson's own outlook is in its most general features that of St. Augustine. Professor Childe's strikingly resembles that of Lucretius; for him, as for the Epicurean, 'history, with its prelude pre-history, becomes a continuation of natural history', and by natural history he means the record of the 'evolution of living creatures as the result of natural selection'.[1] This difference has its manifest effect upon the more general inferences drawn by the two writers, yet each has substantially the same tale to unfold. Mr. Dawson concludes that 'it is impossible to deny the reality and importance of cultural progress. . . . The history of mankind, and still more of civilized mankind, shows a continuous process of integration which, even though it seems to work irregularly, never ceases.'[2] While Professor Childe writes in the closing words of one of his books:

[1] *What Happened in History*, p. 7.
[2] Op. cit., pp. xvi, xix.

23

'Progress is real, if discontinuous. The upward curve resolves itself into a series of troughs and crests. But in those domains that archaeology as well as written history can survey no trough ever declines to the low level of the preceding one, each crest out-tops its last precursor.'[1]

It is, however, very necessary to be clear about the kind of progress which is here affirmed to have taken place. To begin with, though Professor Childe is sure that there was progress during the archaeological period, he is (in spite of the statement just quoted) less sure that there has been progress during the period for which we have written records, that is, the last five thousand years. Within this period, he writes,

'the picture presented is frankly chaotic; it is hard to recognize in it any unifying pattern, any directional trends. Archaeology surveys a period a hundred times as long. In this enlarged field of study it does disclose general trends, cumulative changes proceeding in one main direction and towards recognizable results.'[2]

Furthermore it must be remembered that the pattern of progress thus revealed is in part a pattern imposed upon the facts by the mind of the historian, in much the same way as the so-called laws of nature are often said nowadays to be patterns imposed upon the facts by the mind of the scientist. It is a pattern obtained by an arrangement —the arrangement which Comte, in himself making use of it, called 'the happy artifice of Condorcet'—whereby the story is made to pass from one culture to another, and from one part of the world to another, the culture and region selected to represent each period being the culture

[1] *What Happened in History*, p. 252.
[2] Op. cit., p. 7.

and region which were at that time most advanced.[1] In Professor Childe's words:

'At the worst the archaeologist can turn from the ruins of Mycenaean Greece to the flourishing Phoenician cities and Assyrian palaces, from the wasted towns of Roman Britain to Damascus and Baghdad.'[2]

Over shorter periods there is, of course, evidence of progress in the culture of certain single regions, in the sense that during such a select period the tendency is on the whole upwards, in spite of intermediate regressions. But we can speak of history as a whole disclosing a pattern of progress only if we are allowed to choose what cultures shall be representative of each age. Only in a very limited sense, then, can we say that the race as a whole has progressed. In Africa and Australia there are tribes still living

[1] We do not imply that there is anything illegitimate in such an artifice, but only that its nature should be recognized. Indeed it will be part of our later argument that apart from *some* principle of selection the historian is even more impotent than the natural scientist. 'In historical and kindred studies', writes Professor H. A. Hodges, '. . . both the choice of the subject-matter and the presentation of results are determined by our pre-existing ideas of what is worth while in human life. Those events are found interesting which have notably helped or hindered the realization of what is worth while, and in describing them it is this aspect which we keep to the fore. This does not mean that there are no objective facts in history. There are innumerable facts about dates and documents and all sorts of details, and even a fair number of generalizations about which no one has any doubt. But these are the historian's raw materials, not his finished results. It is when he puts these facts together and tells his story as a whole that his preferences begin to show, and they cannot but appear in what he selects for use and in his manner of presenting it. Two historians dealing with the same period cannot possibly tell the same story, if their moral, political and religious principles are different.'—*Objectivity and Impartiality* (University Pamphlets, 1946), p. 13.

[2] *Progress and Archaeology*, p. 109.

in the Stone Age; and of many, perhaps most, cultures it is true that only a small oligarchic minority reaped any benefit from such progress as was made, the enslaved majority being even less fortunate than they were before. What can probably be said with confidence is that in each succeeding age there was in *some* part of the world a culture which had inherited much of the progress made by the most advanced culture of the preceding age and made it the foundation for some further progress such as benefited at least the upper strata of society.

But we must ask, Progress in what? The archaeologists are clear regarding at least the main part of the answer. It was essentially progress in such an understanding of man's physical environment as led to increasing control over it. It was therefore progress in the adjustment of external nature to man and of man to external nature— the two are very difficult to distinguish. Professor Childe writes:

'The progress that archaeology can confidently detect is progress in material culture, in equipment. By its improvement human societies have with increasing success adapted themselves to their various environments and later adapted their environments to their own changing needs.'[1]

What we have here to do with is progress towards more and better food, more and better shelter, more and better clothing, more and better care of bodily health; such being in its turn dependent on the discovery of better raw materials, on the invention of better tools, better methods of tilling, weaving, etc. This, according to Professor

[1] *Progress and Archaeology*, p. 109.

Childe, is 'what happened in history'. Archaeology, he tells us, has recently revolutionized the writing of history, not only in immensely prolonging the period it covers, but also in altering its content:

'Archaeology is largely concerned with practical everyday things, contrivances and inventions like houses, drains, axes and internal-combustion engines that in themselves have affected the lives of far more people, and that far more profoundly, than any battle or conspiracy, but that formerly seemed beneath the dignity of scholarly history.'[1]

It has been amusingly said by another that 'Archaeological remains are the dry bones of history; a wide scope is allowed to those who endeavour to reproduce the pulp.'[2] But Professor Childe is suspicious of this endeavour, and hardly embarks upon it. He would probably hold that the safest guide to the history of our own period would be the diligent examination, not of our written documents, but of our scrap-heaps and dumps of disused motor cars. He tells us that

'A culture is precisely the sum total of its weapons, tools, houses, vehicles and other things of the sort just examined that were used by a single people. Cultures and their constituents are thus strictly comparable to the bodily "adaptations to the environment" that distinguish varieties and species of animals from one another.'[3]

§ 8

To sum up: the progress which is certainly discernible

[1] Ibid., p. 2.
[2] Sir James Crichton Browne, *From a Doctor's Notebook* (1937).
[3] *Progress and Archaeology*, p. 56.

in history, as we move onwards in time from the Old Stone Age to our own age, selecting in each age the culture at that time most advanced—

> Last week in Babylon,
> Last night in Rome.
> Morning, and in the crush
> Under Paul's dome; . . .
> Off to some city
> Now blind in the womb.
> Off to another
> Ere that's in the tomb—[1]

is progress in such an understanding by man of his physical environment as enables him at the same time better to adjust himself to it and better to manipulate it for the satisfaction of his own bodily needs. The fact of such progress and a few details of it were known to the Greeks and Romans in the later classical period; their knowledge was inherited by the culture of the West; while a further wealth of detail has been accurately filled in by the historians and pre-historians of the modern period.

But is it *only* concerning progress in technical knowledge and skill that a unanimous verdict is thus returned? Is there not at least discernible a progress in such understanding of the corporeal world as is not in this way narrowly aimed at utilitarian application? And is there not also a progress in some kinds of knowledge other than that of the corporeal world?

In the development of mathematical and astronomical knowledge in the West since the time of the Greeks we

---

[1] Ralph Hodgson, 'Time, you old Gipsy-man'.

28

undoubtedly do find such gradual disengagement of the mind from a merely utilitarian interest in the physical. Behind Greek mathematics there lay that of the ancient Egyptians and Babylonians, but it is commonly held that this was of the strictly applied kind. This is strongly emphasized by Professor Childe, who insists that we have here to do only with rules of thumb and not with the deduction of theorems.

'Mathematics is as obviously a consequence of the economic needs of the urban revolution as is writing. . . . It must not be supposed that ancient societies were interested in infinite length or empty spaces. Their abstractions were limited by practical interests.'

'Nor do the mathematical texts ever enunciate a general rule or formula. No rule is stated for finding the area of a rectangle or a circle. . . . The mathematical texts, in fact, consist entirely of concrete problems of the sort likely to arise in real life. . . . Indeed it looks as if the research they disclose was really limited in its scope by consciously conceived possibilities of practical application. In any case, no attempt was made to generalize the results.'[1]

Professor Childe does not deny that the scribes responsible for such texts may have found some intrinsic satisfaction in their mathematical virtuosity, quite apart from its practical usefulness. 'The examples', he tells us, '. . . give the impression that scholars in high centres of learning were setting themselves problems just to see what they could do neatly.'[2] But he does not seem to set much store by this new kind of satisfaction as giving promise of greater things to come. He himself seems to find no value in the advance of knowledge other than a

[1] *Man Makes Himself*, pp. 193 f, 210 f.
[2] Ibid., p. 210.

29

strictly utilitarian one. In another of his books he writes:

'The charge is commonly levelled against Oriental [i.e., Near and Middle Eastern] science that it was inspired by purely practical aims and not by a "divine curiosity" as to the "essence" of things. But the aim of science is surely to amass and systematize knowledge that society can use to control events in the external world, in fact to operate more efficiently on nature; the best test of the "truth" of scientific laws would seem to be their success in so doing.'[1]

There is, however, no need at all to follow him in this judgement, which is obviously in no sense dictated by his archaeological erudition but only by his positivist pre-suppositions. We may therefore allow ourselves to rejoice that within our own tradition of learning from the time of the Greeks downwards there has been a growth, if by no means a steady growth, of generalized and deductive mathematical knowledge such as has been valued for other than merely utilitarian ends. Moreover it must be borne in mind that with the appearance of such pure mathematics we are introduced not merely to a new kind of interest in the physical world, namely an interest dissociated from our desire to control, but also to a quite different sphere of knowledge. For pure mathematics is not in itself knowledge of the physical world at all, but deals with entities that do not there exist, such as points that have no magnitude, lines that have no thickness and parallels that never meet. 'Mathematics', says Professor Whitehead, 'is thought moving in the sphere of complete abstraction from any particular instance of what it is talking about'; and moreover, 'we can have no *a priori* certainty that we are right in believing that the observed

[1] *What Happened in History*, p. 120.

entities in the concrete universe form a particular instance of what falls under our general reasoning'.[1]

On the other hand, it must be emphasized not only that this new kind of knowledge is a very late emergent but also that it has been practised only by those coming under the direct influence of a single tradition, namely the Hellenic. And it is even more important to note that both in its Pythagorean and Platonic origins and in many phases of its later development it was closely associated with certain definite spiritual interests and ontological conceptions of a religious or quasi-religious kind. If on one side mathematics has affinities with the technical control of the physical environment, its affinities on the other side are with man's need of adjustment to ultimate being.

The same duality of aspect manifests itself in another sphere in which a certain progress will be universally admitted to have taken place. Within the period of history for which we have written records, as distinct from telltale rubbish-heaps and the like, there has certainly been a growth in the knowledge of history itself, this very invention of writing endowing the race with a progressively extended memory of its own past fortunes. But again 'knowledge of history' may mean two things; it may mean mere accumulated knowledge of the occurrence of past events, or it may mean some interpretation of these events which enables us to distinguish the significant among them from the trivial. It is only of the former, however, that we can affirm a cumulative advance from one generation to

[1] *Science and the Modern World*, p. 32 f.

another, and from one culture to another, over the whole period. The latter is always closely dependent on ultimate spiritual outlook, and changes radically as that outlook changes, so that little or nothing of it may be carried over from one cultural tradition to another.

If, however, we look once again at the awareness of progress which, in however various degrees, is common to Thucydides, Lucretius, Seneca, St. Augustine and our modern archaeologists and historians, one further element seems certainly to be discernible in it, namely, progress in the organization of society. Yet once again we must consider carefully what such progress amounts to. Does it mean that, as time has gone on, society has been organized in accordance with better ideals, or only that men have learned better how to achieve the kind of social organization which in each succeeding age they have happened to want? Has there been a gradual improvement in social standards, or only an improvement in social techniques? A careful sociologist like the late Dr. Karl Mannheim would commit himself only to the latter. 'Science and technique, including the social techniques, follow an upward line,' he writes. 'The error of the philosophy of progress was that it transferred that pattern of historical development, i.e., the idea of rectilinear rise, to the evolution of the moral consciousness. . . .'[1] On the

---

[1] *Diagnosis of Our Time* (1943), p. 122. Dr. Mannheim adds the words 'and of culture'. This, however, may confuse us. Culture for Dr. Mannheim has a predominantly ethical and spiritual meaning; it is not, as for Professor Childe, 'the sum-total of its weapons, tools, houses, vehicles. . . .' The word in Dr. Mannheim's usage translates the German *Kultur* as distinct from *Zivilisation*; but English archaeologists make less use of that distinction.

whole we gather the same impression not merely from Lucretius but from our own archaeologists; it is in the technique as distinct from the ethics of the social life that they confidently report advance. What does this mean? We may answer that if a cultural technique is a common pattern of adjustment towards one's environment, then a social technique will be a common adjustment towards one's human environment. As we pass from the age of the hunters to that of the peasants, and then to that of the city dwellers, life becomes more complicated. Technical social advance will then mean increasing ability to adapt the arrangement of society to this growingly complex situation. In what the historians of culture have to tell us about the successive appearance of tribal chieftainship, tyranny, oligarchy, aristocracy, etc., this element figures prominently. Indeed some have thought that the changing patterns of social organization have depended simply on the size of the social unit requiring to be organized. Dr. R. R. Marett writes:

'At a guess . . . I am disposed to accept [the] general principle that, on the whole and in the long run, during the earlier stages of human evolution, the complexity and coherence of the social order follow from the size of the group; which, since its size in turn follows upon the mode of the economic life, may be described as the food-group.'[1]

It would be generally conceded that an important part of what we mean by social progress is the extension of positive social relationships to ever larger units, as from the phratry to the tribe, from the tribe to the nation, and from the nation to the world community. During the later

[1] *Anthropology* (1912), p. 159.

periods this movement has been definitely influenced by ethical and theological ideas of the unity and common brotherhood of mankind, and it is likely that in the earlier periods also there were intermingling influences of the same general kind. Hence Dr. Marett concludes that 'social organization seems to face in both directions at once, and to be something half-way between a spiritual and a physical manifestation'.[1]

The spiritual, in this wide usage of the term, may be taken to embrace morals, aesthetic taste and religious worship. We have found no encouragement either in the testimony of the ancients or in that of our modern pre-historians for supposing that men have grown progressively more moral. As for changing tastes in art, Lucretius and St. Augustine knew something about them, and we now know very much more. But the most careful of our archaeologists are exceedingly wary of speaking of progress in this sphere. 'The most surprising and celebrated aspect of Palaeolithic cultures', says Professor Childe, 'is the artistic activity of the hunters. . . . In many instances their products are in themselves of high artistic merit. Great modern artists like the late Roger Fry, admire cave-paintings, not as curiosities, but as masterpieces.'[2] There has, of course, been immense advance in

[1] Ibid., p. 155. The reader may be referred also to Mr. Arnold Toynbee's argument that there is no evidence of a positive correlation between progress in technique and social progress, and to the many instances he cites in which (a) techniques have improved while there has been social stagnation or regress, or (b) techniques have remained stationary, while society has been moving either forward or backward.—*A Study of History*, Vol. III, 'The Nature of the Growths of Civilizations'.

[2] *Man Makes Himself*, p. 60.

craftsmanship, deriving from the discovery of new materials and the invention of new tools and processes. That, however, is something quite different from aesthetic taste and the appreciation of beauty. Thus artistic achievement, no less than social organization, seems to face in both directions at once and to have a spiritual as well as a physical aspect; but while the physical aspect manifests a progress that keeps pace with the progress of technical skill in other spheres, the spiritual aspect does not progress in a rectilinear sense, but rather changes radically from one tradition to another.

As for religion itself, it bulks largely, perhaps more largely than anything else, both in Lucretius's account and in the account given by our contemporary pre-historians. It represents a very large part of 'what happened in history' according to Professor Childe. But it would not appear that in either account we read of religious *progress*. Both for Lucretius and for Professor Childe true progress, so far as it concerns religion at all, seems to have its endresult in the complete disappearance of all religion. Lucretius's most frequently quoted line, *Tantum religio potuit suadere malorum*[1]—'To so much that is evil could religion prompt men'—provides the text for all he has to say on this matter. But Professor Childe recognizes that religion, though apparently having no intrinsic worth or truth, had a certain stimulating effect on cultural progress in addition to its deterrent effect. He writes:

'The superstitions man devised and the fictitious entities he imagined were presumably necessary to make him feel at home in his environ-

[1] *De rerum natura*, i. 101.

ment and to make life bearable. Nevertheless the pursuit of the vain hopes and illusory short cuts suggested by magic and religion repeatedly deterred man from the harder road to the control of Nature by understanding. . . . Magic and religion constituted the scaffolding needed to support the rising structure of social organization and of science. Unhappily the scaffolding repeatedly cramped the execution of the design and impeded the progress of the permanent building. It even served to support a sham façade behind which the substantial structure was threatened with decay.'[1]

This, of course, is orthodox Positivism, in accordance with Comte's teaching that the theological and metaphysical stages are necessary to the emergence of the positive stage in human development, but are nevertheless entirely superseded by it. It corresponds in part also to the argument of Sir James Frazer's book, *Psyche's Task, A Discourse on the Influence of Superstitions on the Growth of Institutions.*

What appears to be true is that religious systems, including not only the institutional side of them but to some extent even their dogmatic formulations, are partly determined by social conditions. There are, therefore, aspects of religion which change with changing social techniques, and if (as we have been led to suppose) history discloses a progress in social techniques, there must have been a concomitant development of religious forms. It will be found that in most of the attempts made during the course of the last century to establish an 'evolution of religion' in the world, the successive stages are made to correspond to successive organizations of society; we have, for instance, the sequence of tribal, national and

[1] *Man Makes Himself,* p. 236.

universal religion. It is, however, a nice question which of the two series of changes is determinant and which consequent; and in any case it is clear that the profoundest and genuinely constitutive aspects of religious systems are in no sense sociologically determined and do not vary directly in accordance with social conditions, but derive from quite different sources. Had we found evidence of continuous progress in the strictly moral aspects of social life, it would have been natural to associate this very closely with a progress in religious ideas and attitudes; but since the progress we have noted is only in the technique of social life, we cannot speak of a concomitant development in the knowledge and service of God.

'Some nations wax and others wane', wrote Lucretius in other lines that are among his most celebrated, 'and in a short space of time the generations of things living are changed and, like runners, hand on from each to each the torch of life.'[1] What then is this torch that has been passed from culture to culture, growing ever brighter between the Old Stone Age and our own? We have found it principally to consist in an increasing understanding by man of his physical environment, an increasingly successful adjustment to that environment and at the same time a gradually improving technique of control over it; but also, and concomitantly, in advancing social techniques leading to a better adjustment with his human environment. On the other hand, such advance as we have with any confidence been able to note in the realms of religion, morality, the sense of beauty, artistic creation, historical

[1] *De rerum natura*, ii. 77 ff.

knowledge and even pure mathematics, has concerned only those less profound aspects of them which are sociologically conditioned and not their spiritual essence. Spiritual advance may be discerned within particular cultural traditions, but hardly as passing continuously from one such tradition to another.

After dealing briefly with this matter in his fine essay, *Religio Grammatici*, Dr. Gilbert Murray goes on:

'You will perhaps say that I am still denying the essence of human Progress; denying the progress of the human soul, and admitting only the sort of progress that consists in the improvement of tools, the discovery of new facts, the recombining of elements. As to that I can only admit frankly that I am not clear. I believe we do not know enough to answer.'[1]

This states precisely the issue which has engaged us in the present chapter. Nobody seems very clear about it, but is this really because we do not know enough? It seems to be rather that our efforts to assess the empirical evidence for progress are disturbed by the simultaneous presence in our minds of at least some remnants of a faith in progress which rests on other than empirical grounds.

[1] Op. cit. (1918), as reprinted in the same author's *Essays and Addresses* (1921), p. 21.

CHAPTER II

PATTERNS OF EVENTS

§ 9

'As to Progress,' writes Dr. Gilbert Murray again, 'it is no doubt a real fact. To many of us it is a truth that lies somewhere near the roots of our religion.'[1] With progress as an observable fact we have dealt at some length. It is to the quasi-religious faith in progress that we must now turn our attention.

That the two are different becomes clear when we reflect that the former is mainly concerned with the past and the latter with the future. It is true that the former has a certain limited bearing on the future also, since the theory of probability yields a reasonable measure of expectation that a pattern discernible in history from the Stone Age onwards is not going to come to a sudden end just in our own time. But we cannot on empirical grounds reach any certainty of this; nor can we reach even a probability that the pattern will continue to manifest itself throughout a future indefinitely continued. Yet it cannot be doubted that some kind of certain assurance of at least the possibility either of indefinitely continued progress, or of its culmination in a perfected state of society, has been part of the substance of the belief we are investigating.

The difference between this quasi-religious faith in progress and the mere factual recognition of it as empirically

[1] Op. cit., p. 19.

verifiable comes out equally when we reflect that the latter hardly extends beyond the technical aspects of life, whereas the former would be stultified if it did not fully cover also such moral and spiritual goods as are held necessary to the attainment of human perfection.

It is clear, then, that the modern belief in progress is no mere inductive generalization reached through the dispassionate contemplation by scientific historians of the past fortunes of our race. It does indeed delight to find support in the dispassionate study of history, and in most minds suffers grave embarrassment when no such support is forthcoming, these finding it difficult to maintain in face of an evident absence of progress throughout the long ages of the past. In most minds, but not in all; for, as we shall see later, some of the most confident prophets of future progress have had nothing but disparagement for the past history of the race. In either case, however, the belief itself has manifestly some deeper root than this empirical one. It is essentially a philosophy of life; and like all philosophies of life, it does duty for a religion; and like all philosophies and all religions, its deepest root is in certain *a priori* presuppositions which may receive welcome support from experience *a posteriori*, or alternatively be troubled by the lack of it, but are themselves beyond the reach of the discursive understanding.

This point was well argued by T. H. Green in the lectures he gave at Oxford as Whyte's Professor of Moral Philosophy between 1877 and 1882 and which were published after his death under the title *Prolegomena to Ethics*. He wrote:

'It is not, of course, to be denied that the facts of human life and history put abundant difficulties in the way of any theory whatever of human development, as from the less to the more perfect kind of life, in distinction from mere generalizations as to the nature of the changes which society has undergone. If it were not for certain demands of the spirit which is ourself, the notion of human progress could never occur to us. But these demands, having a common ground with the apprehension of facts, are not to be suppressed by it. . . . In order to satisfy the idea which sets us upon the search for development, we should be able to . . . view the world, including human history, as a whole throughout which there is a concerted fulfilment of possibilities. This we cannot do; but neither our inability to do it nor the appearance of positive inconsistency between much that we observe and any scheme of universal development, can weaken the authority of the idea, which does not rest on the evidence of observation but expresses an inward demand for the recognition of a unity in the world answering to the unity of ourselves—a demand involved in that very self-consciousness which . . . alone enables us to observe facts as such.'[1]

But the philosophy of life with which we are here concerned is, unlike some others, essentially a philosophy of history. The light and solace it offers derive entirely from a way of regarding the historical scene, past, present and future. One approach to the understanding of it, and the most hopeful, is therefore to set it in contrast with other and earlier philosophies of history, noticing resemblances and differences, and striving especially to see what genetic relations it has with any of them. To this task we shall have to devote both the present chapter and the one following.

[1] *Prolegomena to Ethics* (1883), § 186.

§ 10

The number of alternative 'philosophies' of history which have exercised any important hold upon the minds of men is not very great, or at least is capable of reduction to some four or five principal types.[1] It has been said already that savage societies have no conception of historical change at all. The tribal memory seldom extends more than a few generations backwards, so that men have no knowledge of things having ever been substantially different from what they are now. Nor do they know much of the life of any tribe save their own, so that their own familiar way of life is taken for granted as the only possible one. The course of history, never consciously reflected on, is thus implicitly assumed to manifest a flat uniformity. Men may come and men may go, but the old life remains and does not vary. This is true of the peoples who were still living in the Stone Age when modern exploration first found them out, and is likely also to have been true of our own ancestors.

In contrast with such rude cultures the earliest of the great civilizations of the ancient world—from the beginning of the third pre-Christian millennium or perhaps from the middle of the fourth—are notable for their much longer historical memory. This is due in large part to the discovery of the art of writing which now made it possible to preserve records of past events, but is also due in some part to the fact that the more settled conditions of pastoral, agricultural and early urban life presented better

[1] See the author's *Invitation to Pilgrimage* (1942), p. 86 ff.

opportunity for the verbal transmission of national history from one generation to another than was available in the age of hunting. There is now a real knowledge of the ups and downs of human affairs, of the changing fortunes of at least one's own nation, of the alternation between times of prosperity and times of distress. The records of more than one of these civilizations give evidence that they passed through periods of assured confidence, but also through periods of pessimistic feeling, when the future was regarded with dark foreboding and the past subjected to nostalgic idealization. Men began to tell themselves stories of a Golden Age now passed beyond recall.

When, however, we pass to the surer ground of the first millennium before Christ, we find ourselves almost everywhere in the presence of a much more definite conception. If to the early hunters the process of history appeared as a straight horizontal line, and if to the first farmers and city dwellers it appeared as a line still horizontal enough in its general trend though in places subject to violent undulation, to almost every one of the great civilizations holding the field at the time of Christ's advent it appeared as a great *circle*—or wheel, which in many of these languages is the same word. All change is now held to be cyclical in nature. At the end of a long period the whole course of things terrestrial will be back again in its original state and then, to quote anachronistically,

The world's great age begins anew,
The golden years return.[1]

After a further and equal lapse of time the circle will be

[1] Shelley, *Hellas*.

43

completed once again, and another new beginning be made, and so on times without number; like a 'continuous performance' at a cinema show.

There is evidence that this doctrine of recurrent cycles was already present in the thought of ancient Babylonia and ancient Egypt, and perhaps it was also present in both Indian and Chinese thought before 1000 B.C. Certainly it came to dominate Indian no less than Babylonian thought not long after that date. The cycle was spoken of as the Great Year—the *maha yuga* of the Sanskrit scholars, the *magnus annus* of the Latin writers. Just as there is a periodic recurrence of day and night, of the waxing and waning moon, and especially of the solar year, so over immensely long periods there is a recurrence of the whole cosmic course of things. It looks as if the conception had arisen in this simple form before astronomy had developed very far, but after the procession of the stars had been discovered, it acquired much greater precision. About 250 B.C. Beros(s)us, a Chaldaean priest at Babylon, translated into Greek the standard Babylonian astronomical texts. His book is referred to by Seneca in the context of the passages quoted from him above;[1] it was known also to Josephus and to many of the early Christian fathers; and though it has long ago perished, much of its content is known to us from the quotations which these include in their own works. Moreover, we are told that the recent successful decipherment of the cuneiform texts has gone far to confirm the faithfulness of Berossus's presentation of ancient Babylonian doctrine. But Berossus informs us that

[1] *Quaestiones naturales*, iii. 29; p. 151 of John Clarke's translation.

the length of the Great Year is to be measured by the time required for the planets or wandering stars to reach again exactly the same position in the heavens which they occupy on any given date. Moreover, he also wrote a history of Babylonia, based on ancient documents, and 'arranged it so that it should fill the astronomical period of 36,000 years, beginning with the first man and ending with the conquest of Babylon by Alexander the Great.'[1] He further tells us that each cycle will be marked by the alternation of flood (when all the planets are reunited under Cancer in such a way that a straight line will pass through them all) and conflagration (when they are similarly united under Capricorn). The same figure of 36,000 years is given for the Great Year by the Persian traveller Massoudi, who paid a long visit to India in the ninth century of our era and on his return wrote an elaborate account of the ideas then traditional in that country.[2] The conception of the Great Year itself is already fully present in the Sankhya philosophy within Hinduism, as well as in Buddhist and Jainist teaching.

It looks, therefore, as if the conception were present both in Indian and in Sumerian thought before making its first appearance among the Greeks; and it is more than likely that it came to Greece by way of Babylonia. The nostalgic backward look appears itself to be as native to Greece as it was to the Indian and the Semitic cultures, yet it is remarkable that in Hindu thought it should inde-

[1] *Encyc. Brit.*, 11th edition, article on 'Berossus' by A. H. Sayce. But see especially Pierre Duhem, *Le Système du Monde, Histoire des doctrines cosmologiques de Platon à Copernic*, Vol. I (1913), p. 69 f.
[2] Duhem, op. cit., p. 68.

pendently find expression in a conception of the Four Ages very closely resembling that familiar to us from the Hesiodic poems. It will be remembered that in Hesiod the Golden Age was succeeded by the Silver Age, that by the still more degenerate Bronze Age, that again by the Age of the Heroes, until finally the Iron Age is reached in which it is our own distressful lot to live. In Greece no less than in India this historical pattern became part of the background of popular thought and was associated (whether mainly as cause or as effect) with a generally pessimistic habit of mind—though Greek pessimism was ordinarily much less extreme than Indian. From Greece it passed to Rome, where it is most familiar to us from the poetry of Vergil.

Hesiod, however, has no doctrine of recurrence. It was the philosophers who introduced this idea into Greco-Roman thought, but it appears among the very first generation of these, and there is hardly a later thinker into whose system it does not enter. In the pre-Socratic period it is in Anaximander and Anaximenes, in Heraclitus and in the Pythagorean school. But it is from the references in the writings of Plato that the conception of the Great Year was most familiar to later Western thought, so that it was usually referred to as the 'Platonic' Great Year,[1] though it is doubtful whether there is anything particularly new in Plato's account of it. 'There is no difficulty',

[1] Cf. e.g. Robert Herrick, *His Winding-sheet:*
    'And for a while lye here conceal'd,
      To be revealed
    Next at the great Platonick yeere,
    And then meet here.'

he writes, 'in seeing that time's perfect number (τέλεος ἀριθμὸς χρόνου) completes the perfect year when all the eight revolutions [of moon, sun, the five known planets, and the fixed stars], each having its own speed, reach all together their original point of departure.'[1] On the basis of Plato's formula this was worked out at 36,000 years— the same figure as was apparently current, whether independently or not, in India and Chaldaea. Aristotle points out an interesting consequence. He argues that if, as he believes, time is really circular, the words *before* and *after* lose much of their familiar significance, and we may just as legitimately say that the men of to-day are living before as that they are living after the siege of Troy.

It is clear that these Greek philosophers do not think of events as recurring periodically within a time that follows a rectilinear course, but think of the course of time as itself circular.[2] Time to them was a function of the primary movement of the universe, which they identified with the revolution of the celestial spheres. They had no idea, such as is familiar to us, that time would go on in the same way even if the course of nature were to come to a standstill, even if the universe ceased to exist.[3] Plainly, therefore, if this doctrine is pressed to its logical consequence, it must result in the idea of palingenesia, that is, the reappearance of the same men and women in

---

[1] *Timaeus*, 39.

[2] This is explicitly affirmed by Aristotle at the end of the *Physics*, Bk. IV. 14. 223b: καὶ γὰρ ὁ χρόνος αὐτὸς εἶναι δοκεῖ κύκλος τις.

[3] Cf. especially Erich Frank, *Philosophical Understanding and Religious Truth* (1945), pp. 67 ff., 82 ff.

each successive cycle of time. This conclusion had been drawn in India, and it was now drawn in Greece by Pythagoras and Plato. Empedocles and Aristotle, on the other hand, had hesitated to affirm the numerical identity of the recurrent events and persons, suggesting that the identity was only one of kind. The early Stoics apparently followed the stricter doctrine, teaching that the same Socrates would again have to marry the same shrewish Xanthippe and drink the self-same cup of hemlock; but among the later Stoics a difference of opinion manifested itself and the debate thus arising continued until the close of ancient Hellenistic and Roman civilization.[1]

During the later classical period Stoicism was the most popular of all the philosophies and it was in its very fully elaborated Stoic form that the doctrine of recurrence held the minds of most thinking men, as we have already observed it holding the mind of Seneca. Here the pessimistic outlook on history was specially dominant, and particularly the thought of the great conflagration (ἐκπύρωσις) which would mark the end of the present Great Year and at the same time herald the dawn of the next in the restoration of all bodies to their original position (ἀποκατάστασις ἄστρων). The Stoic Marcus Aurelius writes that:

'The rational soul . . . traverses the whole universe and the encompassing void, and traces the plan of it; it reaches out also into the infinity of time, comprehends the periodic regeneration (τὴν περιοδικὴν παλιγγενεσίαν) of all things, and realizes that our

[1] The Greek teaching about the Great Year is best summarized by Duhem in his great work already referred to. Most of the details will also be found *passim* in E. Zeller, *Die Philosophie der Griechen*. See also Leon Robin, *Greek Thought and the Origins of the Scientific Spirit* (English translation 1928).

children will see nothing new, just as our fathers saw nothing different; so that in a sense the man of forty years of age, if he has any
sense at all, has, in view of this sameness of things, seen all that has
been or ever shall be.'[1]

But once again it is worth noting that this general pessimistic outlook usually went together not only with the
recognition of, but sometimes even with a certain satisfaction in, the increasing technical efficiency of human
society. Men thought of themselves as living in a degenerate age, with things going from bad to worse, and likely
to continue so doing, yet they were conscious of a certain
pride in the increasing inventiveness which marked their
culture and which would probably continue to mark it in
the future. Vergil no less than Hesiod puts his Golden Age
in the distant past and believes himself to be living in a
fallen age, yet has not a little to say in his *Georgics* and
Eclogues of the triumphs of technical civilization. Horace,
in well-known lines, tells us that

> *aetas parentum, peior avis, tulit*
> *nos nequiores, mox daturos*
> *progeniem vitiosorem.*

'our parents' generation, inferior to that of our grand-
parents, brought forth ourselves who are more worthless
still and are destined to have children yet more corrupt'.[2]
Yet elsewhere he paints a vivid picture of our earliest

---

[1] *To Himself*, xi. 1.
[2] *Odes*, III. 6. Mr. Arnold Toynbee quotes a neat translation (*A Study of
History*, Mr. Somervell's abridgement, p. 248 n):
> Degenerate sires' degenerate seed,
> We'll soon beget a fourth-rate breed.

ancestors as a dirty, inarticulate, illiterate and lawless herd.[1] So also Lucretius and Seneca, as we have already seen.

§ 11

It thus appears that the outlook on history pervading all the great ancient civilizations which we have surveyed was, and where these endure still is, a uniformly pessimistic one. What they knew of the advance of human knowledge and technical skill had little if any qualifying effect upon their general pessimism, since they were without the conviction that such knowledge and skill could alter the essential conditions of human destiny. They believed the present trend of things, when viewed on any large scale, to be a downward one and to be heading for final, though it might be still far distant, disaster. There would then indeed be a new beginning, but in this there could be no ground of hopeful rejoicing, since the new round of things would be exactly like the old, witnessing the same process of degeneration, and coming full circle once again to the same melancholy end. What is to us most remarkable about the mentality of all those pagan cultures is the absence from it of anything like *hope*. 'Remember,' wrote St. Paul to the Christians in Ephesus, 'that when you were pagans . . . you had no hope $(\dot{\epsilon}\lambda\pi\acute{\iota}\delta\alpha\ \mu\grave{\eta}\ \ddot{\epsilon}\chi o\nu\tau\epsilon s)$'.[1] He was writing to Greeks, but the words would have been equally appropriate if addressed to Indians or Chinese, Babylonians or Egyptians. For none of these peoples did future time hold any promise of better things, but at best

[1] *Satires*, I. 8.   [1] Eph. ii. 11 f.

the prospect of wearisome sameness and at worst the
threat of doom.

But if all these cultures were without hope, not one of
them was entirely without faith. However essentially pessimist was the ultimate background of their thought, each
did offer men some refuge from despair. Though the sequence of events gave no promise of bliss, there was nevertheless some possibility of escape from that sequence. Men
could not look forwards, but they could retire inwards
and they could look upwards. In the Egyptian and
Sumerian cultures, where the doctrine of recurrence was
not fully developed, the tragic sense of life is less self-
consciously realized, but here also it is in the soul's present
communion with the unseen world above that salvation
is found. When, however, we pass to the India of the
thousand years before the birth of Christ and to the later
or philosophic period in Greco-Roman thought, we find
that every proposed refuge from despair, every support
offered to the human spirit, consists in some definite way
of escape from the wheel of events. The secret of every
one of the great Indian religions lies in its ability to offer
some release from the *karma* of recurrent existences; and
the same is true essentially of the Greek philosophic schools
and mystery cults, except so far as their teaching included
also a promise of personal immortality. Not even the
complete absence of a hopeful outlook on the future can
throw the wise man into despair, because it is not in the
future that his real interest lies but in the changeless eternal
world. Salvation is therefore to be found in the attainment of a certain inward state of mind which achieves

indifference to the events of the time-series, whether present or future, through steadfast contemplation of the timeless nature of things, timeless reason, timeless beauty, timeless divinity. It is true that not all these phrases are equally applicable to all the religious philosophies we have here in mind, but there is not one of these philosophies that is not somehow included within such a general description. Even for the stoutly anti-religious atomists, for Epicurus and Lucretius, the secret of happiness lay in such a contemplation of the nature of things as made men indifferent to outward circumstances, though they were without the belief, common to Plato, Aristotle and the Stoics, that this nature of things was in itself good and divinely ordered. But apart from the atomists, the adherents of almost every other Greek and Indian philosophy could have joined *ex animo* in the singing of at least one familiar Christian couplet:

> Change and decay in all around I see:
> O Thou who changest not, abide with me.

For them all the secret of salvation lay in what the Stoics called the καταφυγὴ ἀπὸ τοῦ κόσμου αἰσθητοῦ πρὸς τὸ ὄντως ὄν —'flight from the world of sense to pure being'.[1]

It must further be noted that, to those whose hearts

---

[1] Cf. Oscar Cullmann, *Christus und die Zeit* (1946), p. 45: 'Es ist für den Griechen ein unmöglicher Gedanke, dass Erlösung durch göttliches Handeln im zeitlichen Geschehen erfolgen soll. Erlösung kann im Hellenismus nur darin bestehen, dass wir aus dem diesseitigen, an der Kreislauf der Zeit gebundenen Dasein in das der Zeit enthobene, immer schon verfügbare Jenseits versetzt werden. Die griechische Vorstellung von der Seligkeit ist also räumlich, durch den Gegensatz Diesseits-Jenseits bestimmt, nicht zeitlich durch den Gegensatz Jetzt und Dann. Sie kann von der zyklischen Zeitauffassung aus nicht zeitlich bestimmt sein.'

were set not on any changes the future might bring but on a changeless world above, the idea of the cyclical re-currence of temporal events even had about it a certain appropriateness and beauty. To them the circle was the perfect figure, the only line that had no beginning and no end; hence only if time were circular could it be what Plato called it, 'a moving image of eternity'. In creating the universe, Plato explains, God desired to make it as like eternity as He possibly could. He could not make it truly eternal, because no created thing can be that, but in making all the motions of it circular, He enabled it so far to participate in the attributes of the eternal world.[1] Plato adds that God 'rejoiced' in this result, as he himself plainly rejoices in it. Within the terrestrial or sublunary sphere motion is rectilinear, to and fro; in the life of God there is neither change nor motion; but in between the two there come the celestial movements, which are the prime movements of the created universe; and these, though they cannot share the timelessness of eternity, at least imitate its endlessness. It may perhaps be said, there-fore, that wherever the cyclical view of history appears in these cultures, some satisfying sense of its divine appro-priateness is found tempering the element of pessimism with which it must always be associated.

Two modern comments on the Greek view of history may be found illuminating at this point. Oswald Spengler wrote in his *Decline of the West:*

'In the world-consciousness of the Hellenes all experience, not merely the personal but the common past, was immediately trans-

[1] *Timaeus,* 37–8.

53

muted into a timeless, mythically fashioned background for the particular momentary present. . . . Such a spiritual condition it is practically impossible for us men of the West, with a sense of time-distances so strong that we habitually and unquestioningly speak of so many years before or after Christ, to reproduce in ourselves. . . . The Classical culture possessed no *memory*, no organ of history in this special sense. . . . For Herodotus and Sophocles, as for Themistocles or a Roman consul, the past is subtilized instantly into an impression that is timeless and changeless, *polar and not periodic* in structure—in the last analysis, of such stuff as myths are made of—whereas for our world-sense and our inner eye the past is a definitely periodic and purposeful organism of centuries or millennia.'[1]

Professor Collingwood's statement in his *Idea of History* seems in disagreement with this only in making Herodotus, whom he regards as the father of scientific historiography, an isolated exception to this general rule. We may doubt, however, whether his view of Herodotus is really justified. He writes:

'I should like to point out how remarkable a thing is this creation of scientific history by Herodotus, for he was an ancient Greek, and ancient Greek thought as a whole has a very definite prevailing tendency not only uncongenial to the growth of historical thought but actually based, one might say, on a rigorously anti-historical metaphysics. History is a science of human action: what the historian puts before himself is things that men have done in the past, and these belong to a world of change, a world where things come to be and cease to be. Such things, according to the prevalent Greek metaphysical view, ought not to be knowable, and therefore history ought to be impossible.'

'The Greek mind tended to harden and narrow itself in its anti-historical tendency. The genius of Herodotus triumphed over that

[1] *Der Untergang des Abendlandes* (1918); English translation, *The Decline of the West*, Vol. I, pp. 8–9.

tendency, but after him the search for unchangeable and eternal objects of knowledge gradually stifled the historical consciousness, and forced men to abandon the Herodotean hope of achieving a scientific knowledge of past human action.'[1]

It is only when the cyclical doctrine lays hold of minds that have already been taught to place their hopes in the future that sheer and unrelieved pessimism ensues. This apparently is what sometimes happened when, after the victories of Alexander the Great, Greek thought began to penetrate Hebrew soil. The Hebrews, as we shall presently have occasion to see more fully, had been led to find stay for their souls, not in the contemplation of a timeless realm above the process of events, but in the hope of a more blessed future; hence a Hebrew coming under the influence of Greek thought would be likely to be left with an outlook even more gloomy than that characteristic of the Greek thinkers themselves.

> You do not know what hope is, until you have lost it.
> You only know what it is not to hope:
> You do not know what it is to have hope taken from you.[2]

A remarkable early instance of this is probably to be found in the book of Ecclesiastes. The word Ecclesiastes is an attempted Greek translation of Qoheleth, which is the Hebrew name of the book and really means something like 'the Professor'. Its teaching is in some ways more akin to that of the Greek professors than to that of the Hebrew prophets, so that it is difficult to believe it uninfluenced by the teaching of the Greek philosophic schools, especially

[1] *The Idea of History* (1946), pp. 20, 29. Cf. also A. E. Taylor, *The Faith of a Moralist* (1930), Vol. II, p. 327.
[2] T. S. Eliot, *The Family Reunion*, Part I, Scene II.

as its probable date has on independent grounds been set about the beginning of the second century B.C.[1] It is with the following well-known words that 'The Professor' begins his book:

'Vanity of vanities; all is vanity. What profit hath a man of all his labour which he taketh under the sun? One generation passeth away, and another generation cometh: but the earth abideth for ever. The sun also ariseth, and the sun goeth down, and hasteth to his place where he arose. The wind goeth toward the south, and turneth about unto the north; it whirleth about continually, and the wind returneth again according to his circuits. All the rivers run into the sea, yet the sea is not full; unto the place whence the rivers come, thither they return again. . . . The thing which hath been, it is that which shall be; and that which is done is that which shall be done; and there is no new thing under the sun. Is there any thing whereof it may be said, See, this is new? it hath been already of old time, which was before us.'[2]

That is the familiar Greek teaching, yet the tone and temper of Qoheleth's book as a whole is more bleakly pessimist than almost anything found in Greek or Latin literature. Even when the conclusions reached are the same, they are here more poignantly felt. Of all the Greek schools the Epicureans were the most negative in their conclusions, and Lucretius believes exactly like Qoheleth that 'all things are always the same' (*eadem sunt omnia semper*), yet with him in the end there is less heaviness of spirit. Qoheleth writes again:

'I communed with mine own heart, saying, Lo, I am come to great estate, and have gotten more wisdom than all they that have

[1] For the evidence of such influences see H. Ranston, *Ecclesiastes and the Early Greek Wisdom Literature* (1925).
[2] Ecclesiastes, i. 2–10.

been before me in Jerusalem. . . . I perceived that this also is vexa-
tion of spirit. For in much wisdom is much grief; and he that increaseth knowledge increaseth sorrow.'[1]

The result has been very much the same when, as has
occasionally happened, thinkers of the modern West have
been led to adopt the doctrine of recurrence. Like Qoheleth they were surrendering a hope which they had formerly held, or into the tradition of which they had at
least been born, and thus their spirits were darkened by
an additional shadow. Friedrich Nietzsche, whose manner
of writing is so reminiscent of Qoheleth, is perhaps the
best known example. Others, like Otto Spengler and
Jacob Burckhardt, have taught a cyclical doctrine, and
though the cycles of which they speak are not those of
the Great Year but only of cultural epochs within the
span of historical memory, yet the conclusion drawn is
hardly less gloomy. But the recurrences of which Nietzsche speaks are very much like those of the ancients, and
what he writes makes even more depressing reading than
the poetry of Lucretius or the prose of Marcus Aurelius.

§ 12

Only twice in the history of thought has the idea arisen
that history might be tracing another pattern than the
circular one, and in both these cases it was the same general
pattern that was proposed, namely, that of a non-recur-

[1] Ecclesiastes, i. 16–18. For much in this paragraph I am indebted to the
late Dr. Edwyn Bevan's *Hellenism and Christianity* (1921), p. 184, and *The
Hope of a World to Come* (1930), pp. 32–4. Cf. also N. H. Baynes, *Israel
Among the Nations* (1927), p. 142 ff.

rent movement towards the ultimate triumph of good. This is the conception which unites the religion of the Magi with that of the Hebrews and which differentiates them[1] from all other religions and philosophies save those which have drawn some degree of inspiration from them —Mithraism from the one, Christianity and Islam and Western thought in general from the other. When, therefore, according to St. Matthew's story, 'there came Magi from the east to Jerusalem in the days of Herod the king',[2] we have a picturesque meeting of the only two traditions in which such a conception prevailed.

Whether the conception was independently revealed to the two peoples is a difficult and complicated question. In one form or another it pervades both the Zend-Avesta and the Old Testament, but Avestan scholars are much divided as to how far it goes back to the founder Zarathustra himself, and Biblical scholars are almost as much divided as to how far it was elaborated among the Hebrews before the period of the Exile when they were open to possible Persian influence. A resolution of these problems is, however, in no way necessary to our present purpose. The things we need to know are plain enough. It is sufficiently plain that the roots of the conception existed independently among both peoples, one Indo-European and the other Semitic, before either could have influenced the other. It is plain also that in the post-exilic parts of the Old Testament, and in Zoroastrianism from

[1] The attempts of the German scholars Gunkel and Gressmann to find anticipations in certain Egyptian and Sumerian scripts have, it seems, not been found very convincing by historians.

[2] Matt. ii. 1.

the fourth century B.C. onwards, world history is regarded as the scene of a conflict between good and evil, which will certainly result in the final victory of good and in the inauguration by divine power of a final era of blessedness.[1]

It is, of course, entirely from the Old Testament, and not at all from the Zend-Avesta, that this conception has been fed into the later history of Western thought, and it is therefore to the former that we must now attend. When we turn from other ancient literatures to the Old Testament, can we say that the cyclical view of history has now completely disappeared? The answer would seem to be that something of a cyclical idea is still with us, but that there is now no thought of *recurrent* cycles. The future consummation is regarded as a restoration, in some sort of mankind's prime estate, in some sort also of an earlier order of things in Israel. So the Christian Church still sings in a well-known nineteenth-century carol:

> For lo! the days are hastening on,
>   By prophet bards foretold
> When with the ever-circling years
>   Comes round the Age of Gold,
> When peace shall over all the earth
>   Its ancient splendours fling,
> And the whole world give back the song
>   Which now the angels sing.

On the other hand, it must be remembered that it is in the later rather than in the earlier strata of the Old Testament that the idea of restoration occupies a prominent

[1] See especially Bevan, *The Hope of a World to Come*, and Söderblom's article, there referred to, on 'Ages of the World (Zoroastrian)' in the *Encyclopaedia of Religion and Ethics*.

place. The now familiar idealization of our first parents' estate as a *status integritatis* dates from a late period of Judaism, or even from the Patristic period of Christian theology, there being very little of it in the Genesis story itself.[1] What is true of the Old Testament generally is that its doctrine of redemption is always in close relation with its doctrine of creation, the end of history being prefigured in the beginning, and the estate to which man will be redeemed at the last being something of a return to the estate to which he was created at the first. Furthermore, as the Messianic hope grew strong in Israel, the future age on which men's thoughts were set was conceived as a glorified restoration of the Davidic monarchy, and the Messiah himself as 'great David's greater Son'. This, however, is as far as the resemblance goes between the Hebrew and the general ethnic view of history. In the esoteric Jewish literature of the Christian Middle Ages there is indeed talk of cyclical recurrence, of generations of men before Adam, and of a succession of future lives after death, but nothing of the kind is to be found in pre-Christian Jewish sources.[2] For Jewish apocalyptic as for Israelite prophecy the Kingdom of God, when it comes, is destined to last for ever.

It was only after the Exile that the expectation of a Messianic Age came to occupy a prominent place in the Hebrew mind. But it is certain that the forward look was characteristic of Hebrew thought long before it assumed

[1] See N. P. Williams, *The Ideas of the Fall and of Original Sin* (1927), Chapter II.

[2] See the articles 'Transmigration (Jewish)' and 'Ages of the World (Jewish)' in the *Encyclopaedia of Religion and Ethics*.

this definite Messianic form. Mosaic religion is already deeply concerned with the *promises* made by God to His people. There is first the promise implied in the creation story itself, there is next the Noachic promise, then the promises made to Abraham, and then the promise of the Promised Land made to Moses. Even when every allowance is made for the ante-dating of these promises by the prophetic writers, it still remains true that from a much earlier period the nation had been taught to look forward in keen expectancy to a better and even triumphant future. It is very noteworthy that in the eighth century B.C. the earliest of the great prophets appears, not as introducing a new hope of a coming Day of the Lord, but as correcting a too uncritical conception of it which he assumes to be already present among the people. Rebuking the wickedness of the nation he cries, 'Woe unto you that desire the day of the Lord! to what end is it for you? the day of the Lord is darkness and not light. . . . Shall not the day of the Lord be darkness and not light? even very dark, and no brightness in it?'[1] This indeed is the characteristic message of all the early prophets—that the promises made by God to Israel are not unconditional, and that unless she forswears her present foolish ways, the future can hold no blessing for her but only doom; and where the later prophets vary this is only in their clearer conviction that a remnant of the nation will always remain faithful and thus enter into the fullness of the promised blessings.

'The history of Israel is the history of a hope',[2] but it

[1] Amos v. 18–20.
[2] N. H. Baynes, *Israel Among the Nations* (1927), p. 8 f.

was in the promise of the Messiah and in the expectation of the Messianic Kingdom that this hope finally culminated. The Messiah was to be of the Davidic line, and in him the royal house would be restored to its ancient splendour; yet it was no mere return to former things to which the prophets looked forward, but a glorious new era such as the world had never seen. The oppression of the poor would cease, wrongs would be redressed, and judges would rule in righteousness. Wars would come to an end and the arts of peace be pursued in quietness. Moreover, nature as well as man would be renewed. The very soil would become more fertile; the very beasts of the field would lose their fierceness; even the heavenly bodies would shine with an increased brilliance—'the light of the moon shall be as the light of the sun, and the light of the sun shall be sevenfold, like the light of seven days, in the Day when Jehovah heals his people and binds up their wounds.'[1] And in this new age men will turn to God with a changed heart. The covenant relationship between God and Israel will be restored and—in the expectation of the later prophets—Israel will become the divine instrument whereby all nations will be led to a knowledge of the true God.

It is obvious that the guidance of history towards a consummation of this kind must be under the direct control of God Himself. The Hebrews had no conception, such as was afterwards to develop in European thought, of a relatively independent course of nature which determined the future by means of a uniform sequence of cause and

[1] Isa. xxx. 26.

62

effect. The events here spoken of are such as could not conform to any conceivable 'course of nature', and they involve such radical transformation as could not conceivably be brought about by human agency. Yet they are to happen on the ordinary plane of earthly history and in the setting of Israel's conflicts with Egypt, Babylon and Assyria. The scene of them is to be the present world, and the blessings of them are to be enjoyed by a future generation of men during their natural life in the places where they now live.

It is, however, well known that during the last two centuries before Christ this Hebrew hope underwent a very great change. Prophecy gradually gave way to Apocalypse. The Book of Daniel was the first of a long series of books which represented the anticipated consummation in a much more transcendent way. This literature was widely influential, and by all who came under its influence the hope of national restoration under terrestrial conditions is now abandoned. The present order, they believe, cannot be renovated but must be utterly destroyed and an altogether new order substituted for it. For the Book of Daniel itself the scene of this new order still seems to be the present earth, but for its successors it is rather 'a new heaven and a new earth', centring not in the old but in a 'new Jerusalem'. Moreover, it is not now only the final generation, the men still living when the present world comes to an end, who are conceived as entering into the blessing of the Messianic Age, but also all the righteous men of earlier generations from the beginnings of the race onwards, who will rise again from their graves with bodies transformed to match their new condition of life. It is irrelevant to our present purpose to discuss the connection of this change in the form of the Hebrew hope with the decline in the fortunes of the nation during these two hundred years, and its final reduction to a state of political vassalage from which there seemed little promise of escape. It is equally irrelevant to discuss how far the new apocalyptic eschatology was formed under Iranian influence; except to remark that the elaborate scheme of Ages of the World, which we have seen to be present in the traditions of all the other great civilizations, but which was absent from Hebrew tradition until it now appears in the Jewish apocalypses (from the ninth chapter of Daniel onwards), is almost certain to have come from this source. One further point must, however, be noted. Though the promised shape of things to come was transferred from future terrestrial history to an age more properly conceived as lying beyond the end of history, not all apocalyptists were willing entirely to surrender the promise of a future time of blessedness on earth, and hence it came to be believed by some that the final winding up of history would be preceded by a thousand years of earthly righteousness and peace. This millennial hope was carried over into Christianity by our Christian apocalypse, the Revelation of St. John the Divine, and is of considerable significance for the later Christian development.

The religion of the Hebrews is thus from the beginning, and increasingly, a religion of hope. In almost every other ancient literature hope is regarded as an evil thing. It is *ignis fatuus*, the great deceiver. The burden of Stoic and Epicurean wisdom in the West, no less than of Buddhist wisdom in the East, lies in the complete renunciation of hope. The wise man is the man who is as much without hope as he is without fear, the man who is altogether indifferent to what the future may bring. The Hebrew, on the other hand, lived on hope, and the whole orientation of his thought was towards the future. When Abraham believed God and it was counted to him for righteousness, it was the fulfilment of a promise for future time that he believed. Far from being a thing to be avoided, hope thus becomes a religious duty expressed by means of emphatic imperatives. It becomes a sin not to hope.

Furthermore, and as the obverse side of the same fact, it is only among the Hebrews that we find any conception of history as a significant process. Nowhere else, if we except the Zend-Avesta, is the sequence of historical events conceived as leading anywhere or as accomplishing anything. The wheel of occurrences rotates eternally on its own axis, and in doing so achieves nothing and advances nothing. And wherever any contrary idea now exists in the world, wherever history is thought of as having a definite direction, as tending upwards, or as leading to a future better than the present, the influence, direct or indirect, of the Old Testament revelation can be clearly traced.

We can indeed go further and say that the very conception of history, as we now possess it, derives from this Old Testament revelation. The sacred books of the

Hebrews differ from all other sacred literatures in being essentially a record and interpretation of events. The Zend-Avesta is, as we have seen, pervaded by the hope of a victorious ending to the human and cosmic conflict, but even it provides no forward-moving pattern of interpretation of the earthly sequence of events. Where its contents are not liturgical, they are theogonic and apocalyptic, but hardly at all historical. Still less are the sacred books of India concerned with history; for Indian thought history is *maya*, illusion.[1] Similarly for Greek thought only the changelessness of eternity is real, and as such the object of true knowledge, while the historical belongs to that realm of appearance concerning which only opinion is possible. 'Consequently', writes Professor Tillich, 'in Greek thought there is no view of the world as history, even though there is no lack of historiography as a report of the confusion of human movements and as a pattern for politics.'[2] Thus the essence of that discovery of history which the Western world owes to the Old Testament really lies in its differentiation of history from nature. Nature, as we now understand it, is the realm of uniformity, being governed by general laws that keep producing identical and invariable results, while history is the realm of significant change productive of genuine individuality and genuine novelty. In nature the same thing happens over and over again; in history each thing can happen only once. The proper application of the cyclical

[1] Cf. N. Berdyaev, *The Meaning of History* (English translation, 1936), p. 31: 'The Hindu consciousness and destiny are the most unhistorical in the world.'

[2] *The Interpretation of History* (1936), p. 244.

pattern is thus to the world of nature, just as it was first suggested to men's minds by the revolutions of the celestial bodies and their effects on terrestrial life. To make history follow a cyclical pattern is thus to depress history into the realm of nature; and to make time circular is to think it in terms of space. 'One might say', writes Professor Tillich again, 'that in this sort of thinking space holds time enclosed within itself.' But 'the circular line is disrupted in the historical view of being. Time tears reality out of its limitation in space to create a line that does not return unto itself.'

'The line of time has always one and the same direction. It has the character of going on towards something—more exactly, something new. This very fact excludes the possibility of repetition. Each moment of the directed process can occur only once. In so far as being is looked upon as historical, it is viewed as happening once. That which is repeated, e.g., the biological or psychological or individual types, comprises the unhistorical element of being. The type essentially belongs to space. The sequence of their appearance affects them only outwardly. In having only one direction, in producing things only once without repetition, time tears itself away from space, history from nature.'[1]

§ 13

This Hebrew conception of history was inherited by Christianity. The New Testament revelation emerges out of the background of Hebrew prophecy and Jewish apocalyptic, and only against that background can it be historically understood. It is indeed a revelation in the fullest sense, creative of novelty, and working the most

[1] Op. cit., pp. 244–6.

radical change of outlook that our race has known. The change was not due, however, to the replacement of the Hebrew pattern of history by another and different one. That pattern had certainly to be adjusted in a number of important ways as the result of what now emerged, but in general outline it remains the same. What is new is the different position within that pattern in which the Christian community now believes itself to stand. The turning-point of history, which had hitherto been in the future, is now in the past—a fact soon to be signalized by a new system of dating which counted all earlier years backwards from Christ's advent, and all later years forwards from it. The new age, of which the prophets had spoken, had now actually dawned, and the Christian Church was living in it.[1]

The very earliest public utterances of Jesus Himself were concerned with the announcement of this changed historical situation. In the first chapter of the earliest Gospel we read:

'After John was arrested, Jesus came into Galilee, proclaiming the good news of God, and saying, The decisive hour (ὁ καιρός) is fulfilled, and the Kingdom of God is at hand. Change your hearts and trust the good news.'[2]

In another Gospel we read:

'And He turned to the disciples and said privately, Blessed are the

[1] 'Das chronologisch Neue, das Christus für den Glauben gebracht hat, besteht nun darin, dass *für den gläubigen Christen die Mitte seit Ostern nicht mehr in der Zukunft liegt* . . . Die Mitte der Geschichte sei bereits erreicht . . . Die Zeitauffassung als solche ist nicht verschieden'—O. Cullmann, *Christus und die Zeit* (1946), p. 70.
[2] Mark i. 14–15.

eyes that see what you see; for I tell you that many prophets and kings desired to see what you see and did not see it, and to hear what you hear and did not hear it.'[1]

On the other hand, the disciples were warned not to mistake this first dawning for the full light of day. When they were inclined to assume that the whole divine event had been completed in the things which happened in Galilee, Jesus corrected them:

'I came to cast fire upon the earth, and how I would that it were already kindled! But I have a baptism to be baptized with, and how constrained I am till this has come to pass!'[2]

'From that time onwards Jesus began to show His disciples that He must go to Jerusalem and suffer many things at the hands of the elders and high priests and scribes, and be killed, and be raised on the third day.'[3]

Only after these things had taken place did the disciples know how truly their Lord had spoken. They understood now that His death and resurrection formed an integral part of that divine invasion of history by which alone the new age could be introduced.

Nevertheless they had still something to learn; for St. Luke records that forty days after their Lord had risen from the dead,

'they asked Him, Is this now the time when you will restore the kingdom to Israel? But he said to them, It is not for you to know the times or the decisive hours, which the Father has set by his own authority. But you will receive power when the Holy Spirit has come upon you; and you will be My witnesses in Jerusalem and in

[1] Luke x. 23–4.
[2] Luke xii. 49–50.
[3] Matt. xvi. 21; cf. also Matt. xvii. 12; Mark viii. 31, ix. 12; Luke ix. 22; xvii. 25.

THE BELIEF IN PROGRESS

all Judaea and Samaria and to the end of the earth. And when He had said this, as they were looking on, He was lifted up, and disappeared from their sight in a cloud. They were gazing into heaven as He went, when, behold, two men in white robes stood beside them and said, Men of Galilee, why do you stand looking into heaven? This Jesus who was taken up from you into heaven will come back in the same way as you saw Him go into heaven.'[1]

That passage, occurring significantly in the first chapter of the book called the Acts of the Apostles, may be taken as providing a key to the whole of the apostolic writings. It introduces us at once to the complexity of the historical situation in which the first generation of Christians believed themselves to stand, and in which the Church has been standing ever since. A full discussion of this situation must be reserved for our final chapter; here it must suffice to indicate only its most general features. The certainty that the crisis of history has been reached is everywhere matched by the knowledge that its consummation is still delayed. The promised salvation has now actually been accomplished, final victory has been assured, the powers of darkness have been conquered, the new age has been inaugurated, and Christians have risen with Christ to newness of life; but the old age has not yet passed away, the defeated powers are still at large, and the fruits of victory have not yet been gathered. Dr. Oscar Cullmann of Basel, who has recently investigated this whole question afresh, expresses the situation vividly when he says that according to the New Testament the Church is now living 'in the time between the decisive battle and Victory Day'.[2] The difficulty of using a single set of New Testa-

[1] Acts i. 6–11.   [2] Op. cit., p. 127.

ment terms to state the matter clearly and unambiguously derives partly from the fact that the day of precise formulation had not yet arrived, so that each writer, and even the same writer at different times, is seeking to express his meaning in such ways as are most readily at his command. In endeavouring to interpret the documents modern New Testament scholarship has thus been greatly exercised as to the relation between the elements of 'realized' and 'futurist' eschatology which they so plainly contain. But the difficulty has its deepest root in the complexity of the situation in which the early Church felt itself to be standing, and a sympathetic study of the New Testament writings can only leave us with the feeling that the actuality of our human situation within these years of grace is here reflected with a realism that cannot be gainsaid. When we pass from the Old Testament to the New, the difference is that the note of fulfilment now dominates everything. Everything is now centred in the incarnation, death and resurrection of Christ. Yet the note of hope and expectation remains, and there is even a sense in which it is stronger in the New Testament than in the Old. In its great triad of faith, hope and love, the New Testament elevates hope to the position of a leading requirement. 'No other religion before Christianity', writes Dean Inge, 'ever erected hope into a moral virtue.'[1] On the other hand, it would be a mistake to regard this hope as a continuance of the old prophetic and apocalyptic expectation.

[1] *Outspoken Essays*, Second Series, p. 178. Cf. also the same writer's *Personal Religion and the Life of Devotion*, p. 52. But it is worth noting that in Christian tradition hope is counted not as a 'moral' but as a 'theological' virtue.

It is not that, but rather a new expectation born of the very fulfilment itself; according to the saying, 'Blessed be the God and Father of our Lord Jesus Christ, by whose great mercy we have been born anew into a living hope through the resurrection of Jesus Christ from the dead.'[1] It need therefore cause us no surprise that, though the fulfilment has been granted, the hope should be greater than ever. This is clearly stated by Dr. Cullmann:

'The Christian hope is not the same as the Jewish. In early Christianity hope certainly appears in its full *intensity*, even in increased intensity, though its object is no longer the centre of the temporal process. . . . This increased intensity finds its explanation precisely in the fact that what forms the centre is not now the object of hope but a historical event that has already taken place. This means that hope for the future can henceforth base itself on *faith* in the past—faith in the decisive battle that has now been fought. What has already happened provides sure guaranty for what is still to happen. The hope of final victory is all the more intense, because the conviction stands fast unalterably that the battle which decides the victory has now been fought.'[2]

To much of this we shall have to return in our final chapter, but one further remark may now be added. We have already noted that a certain sense of present fulfilment had to serve as the single spiritual anchor of those great ethnic cultures and philosophies that were altogether without a forward view. Not only the great religions of the East, but also Stoicism and for the most part Platonism in the West, were saved from the despair which must otherwise have resulted from their hopeless outlook on future time by their ability to anchor their minds in the

---

[1] I Peter i. 3.   [2] Op. cit., p. 74 f.

eternal world above the world of time and change. There is thus a degree of affinity between the thought of the New Testament and the philosophic religions of Greece such as hardly exists between the latter and the thought of the Old Testament prophets. It is indeed an affinity in very great diversity, because the joy of present possession of which the New Testament speaks is not conceived as a joy that has always been available to all men everywhere, but as a joy engendered by an event that has only lately transpired. Nevertheless it remains true that the presence in the New Testament of this new and dominant note provided a limited original correspondence between Christianity and Greek thought, which was lacking in the case of Judaism, and which was to have great significance in the later history of the West.[1] When the sense of present fulfilment and the enjoyment of present blessedness have been held in properly adjusted balance with the hope of better things to come and the longing for final deliverance, Christian piety has exhibited the tranquillity of the Stoic and Yogi without their apathy, and the zeal of the revolutionary without his restless fever and fret.

'I hazard the prophecy', writes Professor Whitehead, 'that that religion will conquer which can render clear to popular understanding some eternal greatness in the passage of temporal fact.'[2] It may be asked whether such a

---

[1] Nor is it any accident that the Fourth Gospel, in which the sense of present fruition is given such obvious precedence over the hope of final consummation, should so often have been the favourite Gospel among those Christian thinkers who had learned most from Plato.

[2] *Adventures of Ideas* (1933), p. 41.

73

phrase does not accurately describe an essential achievement of Christianity.

§ 14

The view of history which was to dominate the thought of the West for so many centuries, and until so near to our own time, was soon filled out on the basis of these apostolic beginnings, if not without frequent shifts of emphasis. The early Fathers of the Church were much alive to the radical opposition existing between their own view of history and the view prevalent in the Greco-Roman world to which their mission was carried, and their long struggle against the Gnostic heresy was in one of its aspects an attempt to protect the former from infection by the latter. They therefore engaged in spirited argument against the cyclical doctrine. At the beginning of the third century Origen wrote as follows in his book *Concerning First Principles:*

'As for those who affirm that worlds similar to each other and in all respects alike sometimes come into being, I know not on what proofs they can rest such an assertion. For if it be said that there will be a world similar in all respects to our own world, this must mean that Adam and Eve will again do what they did before, there will again be the same flood, the same Moses will once more lead a people numbering six hundred thousand out of Egypt, Judas also will twice betray his Lord, Saul will a second time keep the clothes of those who stone Stephen, and we must say that all that has been done in this life is destined to be done again. But this, it seems to me, cannot be established by any reasoning, if souls are really moved by freedom of choice and maintain their progress or regress through the power of their own wills. For souls are not conducted along some revolving course into the same old cycles after many ages, so as to do or desire this or that, but they direct the course of their deeds whithersoever the liberty of their own minds conducts them.'[1]

Two centuries later St. Augustine is still found arguing against the cyclical doctrine and against all the ideas of fate, fortune and destiny, astrological or otherwise, that were associated with it. Eloquently and at great length he insists on the hopelessness of such an outlook and the utter absence from it of any prospect of real blessedness.

'The pagan philosophers have introduced cycles of time (*circumitus temporum*) in which the same things are in the order of nature constantly being restored and repeated, and have asserted that these whirlings (*volumina*) of past and future ages will go on unceasingly. . . . From this mockery they are unable to set free even the immortal soul, even after it has attained wisdom, and believe it to be proceeding unceasingly to false blessedness and returning unceasingly to true misery. For how can that be true blessedness which never has the assurance of being eternal, the soul being either most oblivious of the truth and ignorant of its coming misery or else most unhappily fearing such misery while its so-called blessedness lasts? . . . It is only through the sound doctrine of a rectilinear course (*in doctrina sana tramite recti itineris*) that we can escape from I know not what false cycles discovered by false and deceitful sages.'

It is most interesting to see how troubled he is by the book of Ecclesiastes. Since it is included in the Old Testament canon, and since he believes it to have been written by Solomon, he cannot admit that the cyclical doctrine really appears in it.

'Far be it from true faith to believe that by these words of Solomon are meant those cycles in which, according to those sages, the same whirlings of time and temporal events are repeated, so that, for

[1] *De principiis*, II. iii. 4.

75

example, as the philosopher Plato taught in the city of Athens and in the school called the Academy in a certain age, the same Plato and the same city, the same school and the same pupils, have been repeated at long but definite intervals throughout numberless ages of the past and are destined to be again repeated throughout number-less ages of the future.'

Then he adds impressively:

'For *once* Christ died for our sins; rising from the dead, He dieth *no more*, and death hath *no more* dominion over Him; and we ourselves after the resurrection shall be *for ever* with the Lord.'

After which it is amusing to find him quoting the eighth verse of the eleventh Psalm which our version renders, 'The wicked walk on every side', but which read in St. Augustine's Latin version, *In circumitu impii ambulant*, and which he took to mean, 'The wicked walk in circles'. His comment is:

'I think this fitting enough, not however because their life is really going to recur in the circles (*circulos*) of which they speak, but because their false doctrine itself is of this circular kind.'[1]

It is of the greatest significance that throughout the whole of his long discussion St. Augustine shows himself most anxious to defend the doctrine of creation, and more especially its corollary that through the creative power of God the course of events in time is characterized by the emergence of genuine *novelty*.

'For if the soul is not destined to return to its miseries but is delivered as it had never before been delivered, then something happens to it which had never happened before—something very great, namely, that it is now secure in eternal felicity. But if in an immortal nature there can occur so great a novelty (*tanta novitas*), which neither re-

[1] *De civitate dei*, XII, xiii.

peats anything that happened in a past cycle nor is to be repeated in what shall happen in a future one, how can it be argued that the same cannot apply to things mortal? . . . If then these cycles, by which the soul was thought destined necessarily to return to the same miseries, are finally exploded, what remains more appropriate to true religion than the belief that it is possible for God to do new things such as He never did before, while at the same time manifesting through His ineffable foreknowledge an immutable will?'[1]

In his book on *The Idea of History* Professor Collingwood maintains that 'three great crises have occurred in the history of European historiography'. The first of these was 'the creation of scientific history by Herodotus'— about whose claim to be thus singled out from the other Greek historians we have, however, already expressed our doubts. The third was the rediscovery (but we may think it rather the first discovery) of scientific history by Herder and his followers from about the year 1784 onwards. But 'the second was the crisis of the fourth and fifth centuries A.D. when the idea of history was remodelled by the revolutionary effect of Christian thought'. Prominent among the Christian ideas which worked this change was the Christian doctrine of creation:

'According to this doctrine nothing is eternal except God, and all else has been created by God. The human soul is no longer regarded as a past existence *ab aeterno* . . .; each soul is believed to be a fresh creation. Similarly, peoples and nations considered collectively are not eternal substances but have been created by God. And what God has created He can modify by a reorientation of its nature towards fresh ends; thus by the operation of His grace He can bring about development in the character of a person or a people already created. . . . This was a profound revolution in historical thinking; it meant

[1] Op. cit., XII. xx.

77

that the process of historical change was no longer conceived as flowing, so to speak, over the surface of things, and affecting their accidents only, but as involving their very substance and thus entailing a real creation and a real destruction. It is the application to history of the Christian conception of God as no mere workman fashioning the world out of a pre-existing matter but as a creator calling it into existence out of nothing.'[1]

Many other recent writers have, however, been concerned to make the same point, and to show that the conception of history which has pervaded the Western mind ever since it was first clearly thought out by St. Augustine at the turn of the fourth and fifth centuries, really rests, as St. Augustine believed, on the Christian doctrine of creation and the closely associated Christian view of the nature of time. Professor Tillich writes:

'Historical time is directed time . . . distinguished from physical and biological time. In nature the cyclic movement of time predominates; the end returns to the beginning; nothing essentially *new* takes place. In history directed time breaks through the cyclic movement. Something new takes place and replaces the process of mere repetition. . . . History loses its meaning when it is presupposed that its meaning and value are fulfilled in an eternal world of essentialities, which is either entirely severed from historical development or is only accidentally connected with it. Both in the thought of Plato and that of Neo-platonism history is thus emptied of content.'[2]

Similarly Dr. Erich Frank:

'But the idea of creation also brought about a new interpretation of the phenomena of time which is completely different from that of the Greek philosophers: the subjective time of the soul is distinguished from the objective time of nature. . . . With Christianity,

[1] Op. cit., pp. 46–9.
[2] *The Kingdom of God and History* (in the Church, Community and State Series), (1938), p. 110–12.

however, man acquired a new understanding of time. Here he sees himself as a unique, unrepeatable individuality, created by God; . . . With this idea the magic circle of time has been broken; it is transformed into a straight line which leads into the future towards a definite goal. This is our modern concept of time. It took the passion of a new faith to shatter the idea of a cyclic time. . . . Even the most irreligious person clings to that concept of time which was inaugurated by Christianity as to the most self-evident presupposition of his existence.'[1]

The most noteworthy change that had overtaken the Christian outlook on history between the apostolic age and the time of St. Augustine was the gradual fading out of the belief that the last act in the drama of world-redemption, and with it the end of the terrestrial order of things, was very close at hand. St. Augustine retains, not unfaithfully, the New Testament balance between the joy of present realization and the hope of a greater glory yet to be. He finds a true measure of fulfilment in that peace with God and one's fellows which the righteous soul can even now enjoy; 'but even the righteous man does not live as he wishes until he shall have arrived where he can no longer die or be deceived or injured, and until he is certain of remaining there for ever.'[2] He has therefore much to say of 'the eternal blessedness of the city of God' after the end of earthly history, and of 'the second resurrection' and final judgement by which it will be preceded. He can write movingly of the 'perpetual Sabbath' which the saints will then enjoy. 'How great will be that

---

[1] *Philosophical Understanding and Religious Truth* (1945), pp. 67–9. But see also A. E. Taylor, *The Faith of a Moralist* (1930), Vol. II, pp. 325–30.
[2] Op. cit., XIV. xxv.

felicity where there shall be nothing evil present and nothing good wanting, and where there shall be leisure for the praise of God, who shall be all in all.'[1] But it can hardly be said that he shows any impatience for this *dénouement*. There is among his Epistles a long letter, almost a treatise, in which he recommends to his correspondent a careful equipoise of hope with patience, and lays great emphasis on those New Testament passages which speak of our total ignorance of the time that must elapse before the Second Advent.[2]

Though, as has been said, the belief in the imminence of the world's end had already largely faded out before St. Augustine's time, increasing emphasis had meanwhile —and no doubt as a sort of compensation—come to be laid on the idea of a preceding millennium, when the saints would reign in righteousness on this present earth. But St. Augustine contends strongly against these 'Chiliasts, as they are called in Greek, and which we, literally translating, may call Milliarians'.[3] Their views, he says, would perhaps be tolerable 'if it were believed that the joys of the saints in that Sabbath would be spiritual joys deriving from the presence of the Lord; for I also at one time took this view.'[4] But the Millennarians (to use the now familiar form of the word) believed that the thousand years would be preceded by the 'first resurrection' referred to in the book of Revelation, and would accordingly be a period in which even the physical conditions of life are completely and miraculously transformed. St.

[1] Op. cit., XXII. xxx. [2] Epistle cxcix; to Hesychius.
[3] *De civitate dei.*, XX. vii. [4] Ibid.

Augustine's teaching is that this first resurrection is a spiritual one, and one which has already been accomplished in the souls of believers.

. 'As there are two regenerations, one according to faith which now takes place through baptism, and the other according to the flesh which shall take place in immortality and incorruption through the great final judgement, so there are two resurrections, the one now and of the soul, which saves us from the second death, and the other not now but at the end of the world and not of the soul but of the body, which through the last judgement shall send some to the second death, and some to that life which knows no death.'[1]

This means that the millennium began with the first Advent of Christ and that we are now living in it. Nor is the 'thousand' to be taken as implying an exact count, such as would give us foreknowledge of the date of the end. A thousand is merely the 'solid square' (that is, the cube) of ten, which is a perfect number; and is therefore here used to mean 'the fulness of time'.[2] It is interesting to note how for the support of these views St. Augustine relies especially upon the teaching of the Fourth Gospel with its strong sense of present realization. Nobody could be more conscious than he of the evils of the present age, yet he believes Christians to be already living within the new age. The crowning illustration of this is his famous and fateful identification of the Church with the kingdom of Christ. *Ergo ecclesia et nunc est regnum Christi regnumque coelorum.*[3] In making this identification he does not indeed betray any consciousness of saying something unfamiliar, and it is true that it is already adumbrated in the writings of

[1] Op cit., XX. vi.   [2] Op. cit, XX. vii.   [3] Op. cit., XX, ix.

Clement and Origen.[1] Moreover, it is rather the life of the saints within the Church than the institutional Church itself (which he believes to include tares as well as wheat) that he has in mind when he equates the two terms. But in fact, as von Harnack has said, Augustine 'awakened the conviction, which went far beyond his own expressed view, that the empirical catholic Church is *sans phrase* the kingdom of God, while the independent State is the kingdom of the Devil'.[2] And it was this conviction which was so widely to influence the Middle Ages.

St. Augustine, then, has no conviction that the future of earthly history is likely to be a short one. Indeed he contends hotly against various current ideas to the effect that it would last only 'some say four hundred, others five hundred, others a thousand years', as also against an alleged prophecy that the Church would last only three hundred and sixty-five years.[3] He does, it is true, divide history into a number of clearly defined Ages, and he believes himself to be living in the sixth and last of these. But though his scheme (which often reappears in later Christian writers) is so far reminiscent of the 'Ages of the World' which we have seen to be present in all the great ethnic cultures and to have been there finally associated with the idea of eternal recurrence, it is in reality quite unconnected with them and wholly dependent upon the Biblical history; his Ages are progressive and forward-looking as these were not. And he ex-

[1] See J. Weiss, *Die Idee des Reiches Gottes in der Theologie* (1901), p. 21 f. —a little book of the greatest value for this part of our discussion.
[2] *Dogmengeschichte*, 2nd Edition, Vol. III, p. 137.
[3] Op. cit., XVIII, liii.

pressly insists that the length of the present age is quite unknown.

'The first age extends from Adam to the Flood; the second from that to Abraham, being equal to the first not in length of time but in the number of generations, of which there are ten in each. From then to the Advent of Christ there are, as St. Matthew makes clear, three ages with fourteen generations in each, one from Abraham to David, a second from that to the Babylonian Exile, a third from that to the birth of Christ in the flesh. That makes five. The sixth age is now passing, and is not to be measured by any number of generations, according as it is said, "It is not for you to know the times, which the Father has set in His own power".'[1]

As he looks forward to such generations as may still be ahead of his own time St. Augustine's single interest is in the increase of the number of the saints, and consequently of the Church. Is he optimistic about this? We find it difficult to say. But at least his pages do not give the impression of any particular pessimism regarding it.

§ 15

The pattern which Christianity gave to history, and which provided an intellectual frame for Western culture until at least the time of the Renaissance, is thus an elaborate one. There is enough and to spare of elaboration in such other patterns as the Buddhist and Jainist, but it is elaboration of a different kind, being merely the detailed definition of successive ages within a fundamentally simple cyclic scheme. The orthodox Christian scheme lacks this

[1] Op. cit., XXII. xxx.

wealth of mythological detail but is basically more complex than any other.

For the Christian, terrestrial history is a forward-moving process of a very special kind. It has an *exortus*, a *centrum* and a *finis*, a definite beginning, a middle or focal point, and a definite end. There is first the Creation and the Fall. In the beginning God made man for fellowship with Himself, endowing him with a *status integritatis*, an original innocence which was free from sin but insecure against the temptation to sin. Man at once fell from this high estate and ever since his life has been corrupt—as 'solitary, poor, nasty, brutish and short' as ever a Thomas Hobbes deemed it, and the history of it as much a 'register of crimes, follies and misfortunes' as ever an Edward Gibbon found it. But by the mercy of God something else also is true of man and his history. When we were impotent to redeem ourselves God Himself provided for us a way of redemption. He sent us a Saviour, His own well-beloved Son, Jesus Christ, who took on our human nature, appearing in fashion as one of ourselves, dying for our sins and rising again from the dead for our salvation. This event marks the watershed of history and provides the key to the whole of it, so that the most important aspect of any other event is the relation in which it stands to this centre.[1] This is indicated by the Christian calendar, the system of dating whereby the years and centuries are counted backwards and forwards from the nativity in Bethlehem. The centuries before the

[1] See especially the writings of Paul Tillich; e.g., *The Interpretation of History*, p. 249 ff.

Advent of Christ are centuries of promise. God chose for Himself a people, the people of Israel, and led them through many vicissitudes, through the wilderness into the land of Canaan, through the Mesopotamian Exile to a new restoration, and taught them by His holy prophets to look forward with expectation to the Advent of Christ. This was 'the time of the law', 'the old dispensation' when God's covenant of grace was, in the words of the Westminster Confession of Faith, which will here serve as well as any other, 'administered by promises, prophecies, circumcision, the paschal lamb, and other types and ordinances delivered to the people of the Jews, all foresignifying Christ to come'.[1]

With the Advent of Christ was inaugurated 'the new dispensation' or 'time of the Gospel' when, according to the same authority, 'Christ the substance was exhibited' and new ordinances were instituted wherein God's covenant of grace 'is held forth with more fulness, evidence and spiritual efficacy, to all nations, both Jews and Gentiles'.[2] Yet though the incarnation, death and resurrection of Christ were the events which effectively assured final blessedness to all who now put their trust in Him, as well as to all who before had lived in the hope of His coming, they did not at once usher in the fullness of such blessedness. 'When He had overcome the sharpness of death, He did open the kingdom of Heaven to all believers'; and at Pentecost the promised gift of the Holy Spirit descended upon His disciples to dwell with them for ever. But meanwhile terrestrial history goes on until, after the lapse

[1] Chapter VII, 5.   [2] Chapter VII, 6.

of a period whose duration it is not at all given us to know, Christ will come again to judge the world. This is the end of history, its winding-up; and it will be followed, for all who have accepted Christ's salvation, by the eternal enjoyment of perfect blessedness in the heavenly places. The era of terrestrial history in which we are now living is thus the final era,[1] the era of the Spirit, the era which began with the resurrection of Christ and Pentecost and will end only with the end of the world.

Such is the traditional Christian scheme—as traditionally understood. In a later chapter we shall consider whether any further pattern of forward-moving process is to be discerned within this final historical era itself.

§ 16

All the various patterns of history surveyed in this chapter have a certain *a priori* character. All are in some sense preconceived patterns in the light of which the historical process is seen and interpreted, and no mere empirical generalizations derived from the observed course of events. In some of them such observation seems to have played no part at all, except by analogy—which again implies preconception—from such other observed processes as the round of the seasons and the revolutions of the heavenly bodies. Only in the formation of the Hebrew and Christian patterns does historical experience play a determinative part. The Biblical outlook is in the fullest sense historical. Biblical religion is in its very

[1] The ἐσχάτη ὥρα of I John ii. 18.

86

essence an interpretation of an actual course of events. At the heart of the Christian creed stands something that happened *sub Pontio Pilato*. Yet the significance of this happening, and the pattern to which it is the key, are not held to be discernible by any inspection that is not informed by faith.

CHAPTER III

THE PATTERN OF PROGRESS

§ 17

HAVING now surveyed the various patterns of historical interpretation prevalent in ancient times and other lands, we come back to the pattern most recently developed, the pattern providing what has justly been called the working faith of recent Western civilization, the pattern of progress. It is a much simpler pattern than the traditional Christian one, and simpler also than the cyclical pattern of the non-Christian cultures.

The general conception of things for which it stands has gradually seeped its way into the modern mind during the course of the last two hundred years, and has done this in the most effective of all ways, namely, in such a way that we are largely unconscious of it. Its influence has been of that pervasive kind which not only does not depend on precise formulation but even gains from the comparative absence of attempts at formulation. It is truer of the votaries of progress than of the adherents of any of the great religions that they believe without knowing either quite what they believe or quite why they believe it. And there are very few of us indeed who are not in this way votaries of progress. Even the latter-day intellectual who expressly repudiates all belief in it will soon be found lapsing into language which implies it. He will, for example, slip into using words like 'primitive' and 'old-fashioned' to imply depreciation, and perhaps even words like 'medieval' and 'Victorian' to imply other degrees of such depreciation. Nor will it be easy for him to avoid thinking of the 'up-to-date' as the eminently desirable.

Moreover, when we try to help out the believer in progress by offering him a more precise formulation of what he somewhat unreflectingly believes, the task presents unexpected difficulties. He constantly speaks as if there were some sort of natural law governing the progress of humanity and he derives confidence from his persuasion that, however uncertain may seem the immediate future, ultimate recovery and further advance are thus in some way assured. But if we press him to say whether progress is therefore *inevitable*, he will often be found to hesitate. Another potent ingredient of his modern outlook is then likely to assert itself, namely his belief in the radical freedom of the human will, and he will perhaps tell us that future advance is fully assured only *if* the race takes reasonable advantage of the opportunities at its command. Some, however, will be less hesitant in their answer, believing that there is that in man which will stay him from permanently misusing his liberty, or else that truth and righteousness themselves are such as ultimately to prevail. This conflict between libertarianism and historical determinism not only asserts itself in the mind of the unreflecting progressive, but is a characteristic feature of many attempts to formulate a systematic progressivist philosophy, Marxism being a familiar example. Later in this chapter we shall have to enquire into the historical sources of the two strains, and we shall then be in a better position to understand the difficulty our contemporaries feel in choosing between them.

There is, however, an even more surprising uncertainty in the progressive outlook, which soon reveals itself to careful scrutiny. When a class of students is asked for a simple definition of the progressivist view, it is usually defined as conceiving the sequence of human affairs to follow a line which started very low down very long ago, tends gradually upwards with however violent intermediate fluctuations, and is destined so to continue throughout an indefinite future. The consistent progressive would thus be expected to believe that, as a general rule and after allowing for ups and downs, each successive period of human history registers an advance upon the preceding one. As he looked back upon the age immediately preceding his own, he would be expected to regard it with pride and satisfaction as marking a height never before attained, while at the same time being anxious that his own age should carry this advance a little further; and as he looked forward into the future, he would be expected to envisage a long further movement of advance towards a final goal of perfection which would be reached at some far distant date or perhaps never actually reached at all but approached 'asymptotically'. However, this view of the matter turns out to be largely an academic one. The temper of our most ardent progressives has, more commonly than not, been far removed from any such gradualism. We might perhaps understand that, instead of complacently relying upon the spontaneous operation of the law of progress, they should be impatient for some acceleration of its existing tempo and be anxious that the men of their own time should, as it were, take two steps at once. In fact they have gone much further. [The typical apostle of progress does not proudly stand on one peak and look forward hopefully to the next higher. He does not speak of the existing order of society as the splendid result of a long process of ascent that has gone on for untold thousands of years. He is more likely to speak of it as the embodiment of all that is evil, as being rotten to the core. Nor does he speak of the ideal society as something to be attained in the infinitely distant future, but rather as something just round the next turning and to be ushered in at once by swift and sudden revolution.]

We might indeed be tempted to say that this is not true progressivism at all, but a quite different outlook which might be called Utopianism. Belief in progress, we might say, makes men gradualist reformers, while iconoclastic revolutionaries are working with something much more akin to an apocalyptic philosophy of history. Yet this simple way of distinguishing the reforming and revolutionary tempers does not quite tally with the facts. The great reformers of the past have, as their name clearly implies, been much less concerned with progress than with a return to an earlier condition of things which in the course of time had fallen victim to various corruptions. It is true that certain reformers of the late nineteenth and early twentieth centuries have been genuine gradualist progressives, proud of the level to which society had risen and showing equal anxiety for the conservation of past gains and the exploration of every possibility of further advance. But there are so many minds in which a dogmatic belief in progress resides in unresolved tension with the apocalyptic revolutionary outlook that it would be academic to make this distinction fundamental in our delineation of modern thought.

There is still another curiously discrepant strain in the story of progressivist belief. It will be remembered that Lucretius's purpose in describing the remarkable progress of mankind from savagery to civilization was to establish the Epicurean contention that it had all resulted from the operation of natural forces and the exercise of man's own 'earthborn' powers, with no god to lend so much as a helping hand. The only culmination of this process in which Lucretius himself rejoices is the emergence of the wisdom of Epicurus, and that wisdom was the very reverse of a glorification of the latest triumphs of civilization, being rather a return to the ideal of the simple life. The net result of the progress of civilization would thus seem to be the attainment of an outlook which deliberately repudiates its most typical products and tends to an idealization of the savage state. Hardly was the modern doctrine of progress established in the European thought of the eighteenth century when it began to turn back upon itself in the same way. Jean-Jacques Rousseau provides the best known of several early examples. He shares many of the tenets of the doctrine of progress, being the greatest of all champions of the natural goodness of man and of the perfectibility of human nature, and insisting that such perfection is to be attained by the unaided efforts of man himself, who is distinguished from the brutes by his possession of *la faculté de se perfectionner*. Yet the history of the human race is to him a history, not of progress, but of regress. ⟨Civilization is one gigantic mistake, and the true road to perfection lies in a return to the state of nature. The development of agriculture, of metallurgy, and of civil society are but stages in the process of enslavement which has robbed men of their native rights and liberties.⟩ Professor Bury brings together these two sides of Rousseau's thought by saying that 'He was an optimist in regard to human nature, a pessimist in regard to civilization'.[1] But this does not quite mean that he was an optimist in regard to the individual and a pessimist in regard to society. Rousseau had his ideal for society also, and a belief in its perfectibility by revolutionary means. And it was this side of his thought rather than the other that took deep root in the minds of his contemporaries and was to exercise so profound an influence in the French Revolution. His arraignment of civilization, however, and his ideal of a return to nature, though they have had less direct influence, have again and again reappeared among later writers who, no less than he, were in other respects adherents of the belief in progress—as, for instance, among anarchists and Tolstoians. On the other hand, the ordinary man, if challenged to give examples of progress achieved, will almost inevitably mention those very amenities of civilized life which Rousseau and Tolstoi so much despised.

[1] *The Idea of Progress* (1920), p. 178.

§ 18

These hesitations and discrepancies in the working out of the philosophy of progress derive mainly from the fact that now one and now another strain of the traditional Christian outlook is still influencing the minds of its adherents.

Modern progressivism shares with Christianity, Judaism, and the religion of the Magi the distinction of believing, what has never elsewhere been believed, that human history tends, or is directed, towards the achievement of good. Such affinities as it has with any earlier outlook are therefore all with the Christian; though in the minds of many modern progressives there are combined with their progressivism other tendencies whose affinities are not with Christianity but with Greek and Roman thought, and most notably the positivist tendency whose affinities are with Greek atomism.

Not only so, but it is within Christian civilization and nowhere else that the modern belief in progress has arisen. It has now spread in some degree to almost every part of the world, but only as the result of the general spread of that Western culture which has already for long centuries been habituated to Christian ways of thinking; there is no sign of its *independent* emergence in any other culture. Nor can we for a moment regard this as accidental. Historians have found it easy to trace for us the connection, at practically every critical point, between emerging progressivism and its pre-existent Christian soil. The earliest clear exponent of the doctrine of progress was a French abbé;

many of its early exponents were quite unaware of the extent to which they were innovating on the traditional scheme; and in times near our own the doctrine has been hardly less remarkable for its effects upon Christian thought than for its effects upon those Western philosophies which have in some degree repudiated Christianity. As far as we can see, the doctrine could not have grown up elsewhere than on ground prepared for it by the Christian Gospel.

So far, therefore, as it may be considered to be false, the doctrine of progress is a Christian heresy. Like all heresies it is essentially a lopsided growth. It is the development of one aspect of the received truth to the neglect of other aspects. The Christian interpretation of life maintains itself by a balance of insight, each perception of truth acting as a check upon the too speculative and one-sided expansion of the others. What the doctrine of progress has done has been to disturb this balance. It has been forgetful of much that has been vitally Christian. At a later point in our discussion we shall be raising the question whether it has not at the same time developed one strain of Christian aspiration and insight beyond anything previously attained. If it has, this would by no means be the first occasion on which orthodoxy had learned something of value from the heretics in spite of having to rebuke them for their patent errors. Indeed for the present all that need be implied by calling the doctrine of progress a heresy is that it was a divergence from what had long been accepted as true. Yet, like so many other Christian heresies, its divergence can only partly be accounted for through excessive zeal for one aspect of Christian truth; for a full explanation of it we must take account also of certain extraneous influences playing upon the minds of its adherents.

§ 19

The modern belief in progress is essentially a product, though a late-appearing product, of the movement of the Western European mind known to us as the Renaissance. That movement was many-sided and took many forms, but its distinguishing characteristic is a certain shift in the previously existing relation between men's sacred and their secular interests. St. Augustine had carefully defined the nature of the Christian involvement in the amenities of our earthly existence. We are not, he said, to value them for their own sake, but only to make such use of them as is inevitable, while we wait for the redemption which is to come; and on this distinction between *uti* and *frui*, between use and enjoyment, the whole of his Christian wisdom rests. In this view the succeeding ages had consistently followed him, just as he himself had been faithfully following earlier Christian teaching. This does not mean that everybody throughout those ages lived according to this rule, but only that they knew they ought to, and were ashamed of themselves or shame-faced before others when they did not. But the men of the Renaissance both discovered a new interest and value in the amenities of the present life, and with gradually increasing boldness and conviction defended their right of so doing. Few of them desired to deny the paramount claim of our eternal interests, but alongside of this they put forward a claim for the independent cultivation of our secular interests. They no longer valued the acquisition of knowledge merely as an aid to theological clarification, nor the arts merely as an aid to divine worship; nor were they content to regard civil life as a merely makeshift order of things designed to provide conditions sufficiently peaceful for the Church to continue its evangelizing work.[1] The present life of man on this planet thus acquired an autonomous dignity and importance which had been denied it by the traditional Christian scheme. The idea that this life was a *progressive* one was not yet consciously present, but the soil was now prepared for it and the step taken which made its emergence possible.

It would perhaps have been natural that when interest was thus so far shifted from life eternal to our present planetary existence, the hopeful forward look which had previously been so exclusively fixed on the former would

---

[1] '. . . the State as such can hardly be traced in the Middle Ages. The State is an organization of secular life. Even if it goes beyond its elementary purpose of security for person and property, and devotes itself to spiritual purposes, it is concerned with the development of the spirit in its mortal existence, and confined to the expansion of the mind in the bounds of a mortal society. The Middle Ages thought more of salvation than of security, and more of the eternal society of all the faithful, united together in Christ their Head, than of any passing society of this world only. They could recognize kings, who bore the sword for the sake of security, and did justice in virtue of their anointing. But kings were not, to their thinking, the heads of secular societies. They were agents of the one divine commonwealth— defenders of the Faith, who wielded the secular sword for the furtherance of the purposes of God.'—Sir Ernest Barker in his essay on 'The Unity of Mediaeval Civilization' in *Church, State and Study*, p. 66.

likewise have been shifted to the latter, the new secularism thus leading at once to belief in secular progress. But this movement of thought and feeling was delayed by the significant and well-known fact that what gave sustenance to the first period of the Renaissance was not the cultivation of quite new fields of thought but the recovery of the long-neglected riches of pagan classical culture. Classical thought cannot itself be characterized as on the whole humanistic. In most of its manifestations it was deeply imbued with religious motives. 'I perceive', said St. Paul to the Athenians, 'that you are in all respects very religious (δεισιδαιμονεστέρους)'.[1] There were indeed strong humanist strains in classical thought, as among the Sophists, Cyrenaics, Atomists and Epicureans, in Hellenistic art and in the Roman theatre; and some of the early spirits of the Renaissance found here what they required. But the majority of the humanists found it rather in the main stream of the classical tradition, Platonist, Aristotelian and Stoic. For even in these systems the secular interest had been developed far beyond anything that was encouraged by the Christianity of the Dark Ages, and this earlier development had to be retraversed before further advance could be made. To this day, therefore, the word humanism has a double meaning; it may mean either the love of classical literature or the restriction of interest to the present life of man on earth.

Soon, however, it became evident that this retrospective movement was to be for many minds no more than a *reculer pour mieux sauter*. Then began the heated contro-

[1] Acts xvii. 22.

versy between the claims of the ancients and those of the moderns to which Swift in 1704 gave the name of the Battle of the Books. On the one side were marshalled those who were sceptical of the possibility of any advance beyond the great classical models, on the other those who claimed with Charles Perrault that 'a dwarf on a giant's shoulders sees the farther of the two'. The controversy continued to rage throughout the seventeenth century and was dying down only as Swift published his brilliant, if far from profound, satire. Or perhaps it has not yet died down. Do not the rival claims of a classical and 'modern' education still remain unsettled? In Dr. Gilbert Murray's essay *Religio Grammatici*, from which we have already quoted more than once, the old dilemma reappears in a most interesting form. To him the idea of progress is an article of faith; 'to many of us it is a truth that lies somewhere near the roots of our religion'. Many modern Christians would have to say as much, and would then be faced with the difficult task of reconciling this confession with their essential belief in the finality and all-sufficiency of the faith once for all delivered to the saints of two thousand years ago. Dr. Murray too is faced with a difficulty, but in his case it is that of reconciling belief in progress with his own *pietas* towards the literature of classical paganism. 'I believe', he writes, 'this difficulty about Progress, this fear that in studying the great teachers of the past we are in some sense sitting at the feet of savages, causes real trouble of mind to many keen students.'[1] His solution of the difficulty much resembles that

[1] Op. cit., p. 19.

99

with which many Christians try to adjust their own; and if it halts a little, the other frequently halts no less.

It was only when in the Battle of the Books the tide began to turn in favour of the moderns that the idea of progress was given freedom to develop. For this two thinkers were primarily responsible, the thinkers with whose names most of our histories of modern thought begin, Francis Bacon and René Descartes. Both wrote in the early part of the seventeenth century, the one initiating the new development of British and the other of Continental thought. When viewed from our present standpoint both may seem to belong as much to the medieval as to the modern period, and to have learned most of what they knew from the Aristotelian tradition. Yet each was as eager as the other to acknowledge the worth of that tradition only so far as it was confirmed by their own independent enquiries, and they accordingly rivalled one another, though in very different ways, in challenging its sacrosanctity. On nothing were their hearts more set than on 'the advancement of learning', which to them was the same thing as 'the progress of science'. The most general difference between them, as between the ensuing British and Continental developments, is that the former was more empirical, the latter more speculative; the one relying more on experiment and the other on deduction from first principles. This contrast, however, must not be pressed too far.

The following passage from his *Novum Organum* will serve as an example of Bacon's general attitude towards the future:

'By far the greatest obstacle to the advancement of the sciences and the undertaking of any new attempt or department is to be found in men's despair and the idea of Impossibility. For men of a prudent and exact turn of thought are altogether diffident in matters of this nature, considering the obscurity of Nature, the shortness of life, the deception of the senses and weakness of the judgement. They think therefore that in the revolutions of ages and of the world there are certain floods and ebbs of the sciences, and that they grow and flourish at one time, and wither and fall off at another, that when they have attained a certain degree and condition they can proceed no further. If therefore any one believe or promise greater things, they impute it to an uncurbed and premature mind, and imagine that such efforts begin pleasantly, then become laborious, and end in confusion. And since such thoughts easily enter the minds of men of dignity and excellent judgement, we must really take heed lest we should be captivated by our affection for an excellent and most beautiful object, and relax or diminish the severity of our judgement, and we must diligently examine what gleam of hope shines upon us, and in what direction it manifests itself, so that banishing her lighter dreams, we may discuss and weigh whatever appears of more sound importance. . . . Let us then speak of Hope, especially as we are not vain promisers nor are willing to force and ensnare men's judgement, but would rather lead them willingly forward. . . .'[1]

To represent Descartes we may select the following from the closing chapter of his *Discourse on Method*:

'As soon as I had arrived at certain general ideas concerning physical science and, beginning to put these to the test in various difficult cases, had observed how far they can lead us and how much they differ from the principles in use up to the present, I believed that I could not keep them secret without sinning gravely against the law which obliges us to promote as far as in us lies the general welfare of mankind. For they made me see that it is possible to

[1] Op. cit., I. xcii.

attain such knowledge as would be highly useful for life, and that in place of that speculative philosophy taught in the schools one can discover a practical philosophy by means of which, understanding the force and action of fire, water, air, the stars, the heavens and all the other bodies that surround us, as clearly as we understand the various crafts of our artisans, we should be able to apply them in a like way to all their proper uses and so to make ourselves lords and masters of nature. Nor is this to be desired merely with a view to the invention of an infinity of contrivances such as might enable us to enjoy without labour the fruits of the earth and all the conveniences it offers, but also and principally with a view to the preservation of health which is undoubtedly the chief good and the foundation of all the other goods of the present life. For the spirit itself is so greatly dependent upon the condition and disposition of the bodily organs that, if it is possible to discover any means of making men generally more sensible and competent (*plus sages et plus habiles*) than they have been hitherto, I believe it is in medicine that these means must be sought.'

§ 20

Bacon and Descartes stand on the frontier between medieval and modern thought, but the above passages reveal several of the respects in which they belong to the modern period. Both were by profession orthodox Christian believers, yet both displayed a new kind of concern for the advancement of man's earthly interests. The hope of which Bacon discourses so eloquently is not the hope of heavenly glory, but the hope of such progress in the understanding of nature as will bring about a greater measure of temporal wellbeing. Similarly Descartes concludes his *Discourse* with the declaration: 'This only will I say, that I have resolved to employ the time that still remains to me in life for no other task than that of acquiring some understanding of nature such as will enable me to lay down more assured rules for medicine than have hitherto been available.' Descartes and Bacon both believed that in their time the world was standing on the threshold of new knowledge, and each was as excited as the other by the prospect of the enlightenment which would thus be brought about. In this their temper is already sufficiently different from that of the ages of tradition. But much more profoundly different is their conception of the use which the new knowledge and enlightenment are to serve. During the preceding ages knowledge was valued mainly as food for the contemplative life, but Descartes and Bacon think much more of its employment for the advancement of the temporal and physical amenities of mankind.

Both are thus much concerned with the hope of earthly advancement. The progress they look for is essentially the progress of scientific (in Descartes' case chiefly of medical) knowledge, but their interest in it lies largely in the promise it gives of betterment in man's earthly lot. How far then do they carry us towards the modern doctrine of progress? We can at least say that their thought provides the necessary presuppositions of that doctrine and creates a temper most hospitable to its emergence. But we can hardly say more. Neither in Bacon nor in Descartes is there much sign of a disposition to regard the whole of history as displaying a progressive pattern. Neither was interested to apply that or any other particular pattern to the past, and neither extends his interest to the distant future. Both thought rather of their own time as marking a break with the long-standing traditions of the past, and both probably hoped that the enlightenment they dreamed of would be achieved in the very near future. Furthermore, neither seems to have entertained any illusions about the inevitability of such achievement, each being content to demonstrate the possibility of it and to argue (as Bacon does in the passage quoted) against the assumption of its impossibility. Here, therefore, we have no real dogma of progress, no talk of a law or pattern governing the vicissitudes of mortal affairs.

Perhaps it is not surprising that it was within the Cartesian rather than the Baconian tradition that the dogma of progress made its first full-dress appearances. British philosophy continued to follow the more empirical lines which Bacon had marked out for it, while the Cartesian method of deduction from first principles was carried still further by the Continental thinkers. And we have already seen that the essential element in the modern belief in progress is of a speculative or *a priori* kind, and not such as readily to be suggested by the observation of historical data alone.

The story of the gradual emergence of this belief from the end of the seventeenth century onwards, and of its development throughout the eighteenth and nineteenth centuries, has been admirably told for us by Bury in his book, *The Idea of Progress, an Inquiry into its Origin and Growth*, published in 1920. Bury indeed has done his work so well that it would be lost labour to attempt here to re-traverse with any particularity the ground he covered.

His book is both accurate in detail—for he was a very great historian—and sufficiently complete, though it barely carries the story up to the emergence of Marxism. Such faults as it has are faults of generalization. Bury writes throughout from a positivist point of view, but whereas the doctrine of progress is the central article of faith of modern positivism in general, he professes scepticism of its validity; yet finally, having nothing else to cling to, he comes near to contradicting himself by seeming to suggest that the idea of progress is itself but a stage in the progress of the human mind which will soon replace it by some other and presumably better idea. He also makes too much of the part played by the new sense of the uniformity of nature in corroding and destroying the Christian belief in an active intervening Providence. He himself regards the two beliefs as fundamentally incongruous, and accordingly insists that 'so long as the doctrine of Providence was indisputably in the ascendant, the doctrine of Progress could not arise'.[1] Such an argument, however, proves too much, since any conception of the uniformity of nature which thus simply excluded Providence would at the same time exclude human freewill, and without human free-will there can be no manmade progress. No doubt the 'cast iron' conception of a mechanistic universe, which made its appearance from d'Holbach and de la Mettrie onwards and became so familiar in the later nineteenth century, did rigidly exclude the free action of God and man alike, but no such conception dominated the seventeenth and early eight-

[1] Op. cit., p. 21 f.

eenth centuries. Moreover, Bury does less than justice to the sense of the uniformity of nature already present in the Middle Ages. For St. Thomas Aquinas, as for Plato and Aristotle, the orderliness of nature was evidence of God's control of it, though he did not believe God Himself to be bound by an order which was of His own making.[1]

In addition, it must be said that Bury by no means fully brings out the extent to which the idea of progress is itself a derivation, legitimate or not, from Christian conceptions. Nor does he sufficiently stress the differences between the various 'layers' which we shall in the sequel find ourselves obliged to distinguish as having been superimposed upon the earlier idea during the late eighteenth and the nineteenth centuries.

Nevertheless, bearing in mind these general reservations, we may safely, and most gratefully, follow Bury's account of the gradual emergence of the idea from the end of the seventeenth century onwards. Two successive chapters of his work are entitled 'The Progress of Knowledge: Fontenelle' and 'The General Progress of Man: Abbé de Saint-Pierre'. He shows clearly how it was the progress of *knowledge* that the early exponents of the idea were most concerned to establish, and for Fontenelle he

---

[1] 'This unquestioned belief in order, with its chequered history—Plato and Epicurus, the Gnostics, the Alexandrian theologians, the rationalists of Antioch and Mopsuestia, the Manicheans, Augustine, Calvin—finally started the first phase of the modern world in the sixteenth century, with the unquestioning presupposition that there is an order of nature which lies open in every detail to human understanding.'—A. N. Whitehead, *Adventures of Ideas*, p. 167.

defends the claim of being 'the first to formulate the idea of the progress of knowledge as a complete doctrine'.[1] Fontenelle's predecessors had looked forward hopefully to such a progress, but he was the first to speak of it as being necessary and certain, and as destined to continue indefinitely into the future. He had a strong sense of the invariability alike of external and of human nature, taking special pains to refute the view that the latter is subject to degeneration. He was accordingly able to argue that each generation, having no less ability than its predecessors, reaps profit alike from their discoveries and from their mistakes, so that 'the sound views of intellectual men in successive generations will continually add up'. But, adds Bury, 'this principle, which seemed to secure the indefinite progress of knowledge, disabled Fontenelle from suggesting a theory of the progress of society'.[2] For if human nature grows no worse, neither does it grow any better; and that very invariability of it which ensures the building up of knowledge must at the same time preclude the possibility of moral or social improvement.

But during the latter half of Fontenelle's own long life-time other ideas were beginning to stir men's minds in France. Throughout the reign of Louis XV the ferment of social thinking, which was ultimately to find expression in the Revolution, was more and more making its presence felt, until at last few could be found to take pleasure in an intellectual enlightenment which gave no promise of a betterment of social and governmental ills.

[1] Op. cit., 110.   [2] Op. cit., p. 110.

Bury finds in the voluminous writings of the Abbé de Saint-Pierre[1] the earliest attempt to meet this situation (or rather an anticipation of a situation which was not yet fully developed in his own lifetime) by teaching clearly that the progress of knowledge holds within itself the sufficient secret of ever-increasing human happiness and welfare. Thus what Saint-Pierre did was to combine Bacon's and Descartes' belief that increase in knowledge was the secret of moral and social progress with Fontenelle's belief in the inevitability of the former; so reaching as a conclusion the belief in the inevitability of the latter. Bury writes:

'Between 1690 and 1740 the conception of an indefinite progress of enlightenment had been making its way in French intellectual circles, and must often have been a topic of discussion in the *salons*, for instance, of Madame de Lambert, Madame de Tencin and Madame Cupin, where Fontenelle was one of the most conspicuous guests. To the same circle belonged his friend the Abbé de Saint-Pierre, and it is in his writings that we first find the theory widened to embrace progress towards social perfection.'[2]

In more than one book Saint-Pierre expounded a scheme for the establishment of perpetual peace, advocating to this end an alliance under a single international Diet of all the sovereign states of Europe. In other books he expounded a variety of projects for the better government of individual states, advocating especially the creation of an Academy of Politics on the analogy of the

[1] Not to be confused with that later namesake of his, the even more unpractical dreamer, Bernardin de Saint-Pierre, who is chiefly remembered as the author of *Paul and Virginia*.
[2] Op. cit., p. 128.

existing Academy of Sciences. Towards the end of his life he published his *Observations on the Continuous Progress of Universal Reason* (1737) in which the fundamental pre-suppositions of his practical proposals are set out with some degree of clarity. The efforts of human reason have, he believes, been in the past too much confined to the natural and speculative sciences, and too little attention has been paid to the improvement of social and political knowledge. This is why such spectacular advances have been made in our knowledge of nature, while mankind has meanwhile grown neither any better nor any happier. Yet reason has in itself as much power to stimulate pro-gress in the one sphere as in the other, and if the ablest minds should now devote themselves to the ethical and political problems with as much enthusiasm as they have hitherto consecrated to the solution of merely speculative problems, rapid and continuous progress towards human perfection would be the inevitable result. Moreover, the Abbé believes that this is bound to happen. He is an optimist not only in respect of his confidence in the power of governments to bring about human happiness by legis-lative action, but also in believing that the time had now come when the human reason would actually begin the rapid development of its powers along this new line of advance. Bacon has already laid all the stress on the utility of knowledge rather than on its value for the nourishment of the *vita contemplativa*. Descartes had gone further, sug-gesting that the development of medical science held within it the secret of greater human happiness. But the Abbé's writings display both a much more sanguine outlook than either of these and also an outlook into a more distant future. Bury writes again:

'Here we have for the first time, expressed in definite terms, the vista of an immensely long progressive life in front of humanity. Civilization is only in its infancy. Bacon, like Pascal, had conceived it to be in its old age. Fontenelle and Perrault seem to have regarded it as in its virility; they set no term to its duration, but they did not dwell on future prospects. The Abbé was the first to fix his eye on the remote destinies of the race and name immense periods of time.'[1]

§ 21

Most of Saint-Pierre's contemporaries laughed at his projects, and none took him as seriously as he took himself. Yet in the half-century separating his death from the outbreak of the French Revolution (that is, the second half of the eighteenth century) the underlying presuppositions of his thought came to be almost common ground among the so-called French *philosophes*. The passion for social reform, the determined application of man's rational powers to this new field, confidence in the ability of law and government to bring about an immediate improvement in human affairs, and the combination of these proximate hopes with a still brighter vision of the more distant future—all these became naturalized in the French mind of this period, spreading also to England and Germany.

The story of this development is fully set out in seven chapters of Bury's book. It is also most engagingly, though less systematically, told in Dr. Carl Becker's *The*

[1] Op. cit., p. 136 f.

Heavenly City of the Eighteenth-Century Philosophers (1932) where the general temper of the period is thus summarized:

'Mankind has at last emerged, or is emerging, from the dark wilderness of the past into the bright, ordered world of the eighteenth century. From this high point of the eighteenth century the Philosophers survey the past and the future. They recall the miseries and errors of the past, as mature men recall the difficulties and follies of youth, with bitter memories it may be, yet with a tolerant smile after all, with a sigh of satisfaction and a complacent feeling of assurance: the present is so much better than the past. But the future, what of that? Since the present is so much better than the past, will not the future be much better than the present? To the future the Philosophers look, as to a promised land, a new millennium.'[1]

Dr. Becker's final chapter is entitled 'The Uses of Posterity' and takes as its text the epigram of Diderot that 'Posterity is for the Philosopher what the other world is for the religious man',[2] together with the saying of Priestley that 'Whatever was the beginning of this world, the end will be glorious and paradisaical, beyond what our imagination can conceive'[3]—which is obviously a secularized version of 'Eye hath not seen, etc.'. The thought of posterity had played a considerable part in many ancient cultures; for while there was as yet no idea of a future life for the individual such as could be looked forward to with joy, hope could have no other object

[1] Op. cit., p. 118.

[2] Becker gives the reference: *Oeuvres*, XVIII. 101.

[3] From the opening pages of Priestley's *First Principles of Government* (1768). Bury too quotes this passage, and also from the same pages the saying that 'men will make their situation in this world abundantly more easy and comfortable; they will probably prolong their existence in it and will grow daily more happy.'

than the earthly continuance of the family, tribe or nation. It had attained its greatest significance in that period of ancient Israelite thought when history was already conceived according to a forward-moving pattern but belief in the resurrection of the dead had not yet emerged. God's covenant with Abraham was that he would be multiplied exceedingly, that he would be the father of many nations, that kings would come out of him, and that his seed would have the land of Canaan for an everlasting possession.[1] When, therefore, in the eighteenth century, the belief in the resurrection of the dead began to lose its hold on men's minds, while at the same time the forward-looking tendency characteristic of the Judaeo-Christian revelation had lost nothing of its power, it was inevitable that earthly posterity should once again become the principal substance of hope. The new conception, however, differed from the ancient one in two opposite ways. The hope of Israel was for the continuance and expansion of a single holy tradition; but in the eighteenth-century mind this hope was diffracted in the opposite directions of a diffuse universalism ultimately deriving from a mixture of Christian and Stoic strains, and an egoistic individualism foreign to all varieties of ancient thought. On the one hand, the *philosophe* works with a general (and, it must be confessed, somewhat vaguely imagined) idea of humanity, and his hope is that the race of men will as a whole be wiser and happier in the future than it has been in the past; but on the other hand he counts upon posterity for his own vindication, and his hope is set upon the continued

[1] Gen. xvii. 4–8.

remembrance of his own name. That last infirmity more besets the noble mind of the eighteenth century than that of any previous age. A well-known example is Robert Southey's poem about his library, which ends with the lines:

> My hopes are with the Dead; anon
>> My place with them will be,
> And I with them shall travel on
>> Through all Futurity;
> Yet leaving here a name, I trust,
> That will not perish in the dust.

The excellence of Dr. Becker's treatment of the period is that while he clearly exposes its new attitude to the future, he no less clearly shows that this new attitude is essentially a redisposition of the Christian ideas which it seeks to displace. The dramatic conception of history, the hopeful looking-forward, the belief that events move towards some desirable goal, the dream of a promised land or millennial or paradisaical state, and even the idea of some future court of judgement in which virtue will be vindicated and crowned while corruption is exposed and condemned: not only were these conceptions so much become a part of the general mind of Europe that a philosophy which excluded them would altogether fail of appeal, but even the *philosophe* was unable to think himself out of them.[1] All he could do, therefore, was to

[1] Cf. Christopher Dawson, *Progress and Religion, an Historical Enquiry* (1929), p. 190; 'When the philosophers of the eighteenth century attempted to substitute their new rationalist doctrines for the ancient faith of Christendom, they were in reality simply abstracting from it those elements which had entered so deeply into their own thought that they no longer recognized their origin.'

transfer his hope from the eternal to the temporal scene, to shift attention from the glorified future life of those already born and dead to a possible better earthly life for those yet to be born, to replace the desire for immortality with the desire to influence future generations and if possible to be remembered by them, to transpose paradise from heaven to earth, and to make posterity rather than God the final judge.

A place of some importance in the development of the new outlook on history is rightly accorded by Bury to the Chevalier de Chastellux who in 1772 published his widely influential book *On Public Felicity, or Considerations on the Lot of Men in the Various Epochs of History*. Chastellux's purpose is to establish the certainty of the future progress of mankind. He wants his contemporaries to look forward to the future with confident expectation rather than to deceive themselves with any idealization of the past. But in order to do this he does not display the course of history as a gradual process of advance in which each age was happier than the preceding one; rather does he dwell on the misery of all past ages prior to the Renaissance, dating from that time the beginning of the progress which is now destined to continue. Having concluded his survey he writes:

'As a result of our interrogation of history we find ourselves only too well convinced that the peoples of the world not only have never known true happiness but have never even followed the path that could lead them towards it. . . . But to make up for this melancholy view that we have taken of the past, we have felt coming to birth in ourselves a very sweet hope for the ages to come, and also a very comforting estimate of the present age. We have admired our ancestors less; but we have loved our contemporaries better and have vested greater hopes in our descendants.'[1]

Such a view, like those of Saint-Pierre and Turgot, stands in obvious contrast to that of Rousseau. On the one side there is delight in the advance of modern civilization and reliance upon the ability to accelerate this advance by legislative and governmental action; on the other there is anarchistic idealization of the primitive state of nature. Nevertheless the two strains came together in the events of 1789, for if it was Voltaire and the Encyclopaedists who provided much of the programme for the early stages of the French Revolution, it was the quasi-religious passion of Rousseau that supplied the necessary fire. During the brief years that separated the storming of the Bastille from the beginning of the Reign of Terror it seemed to many that a glorious new era was indeed being inaugurated, when all the resources of government would be devoted with a single eye to the progress of mankind as that had been conceived by the philosophers. A single year of Robespierre's rule did much to dispel this illusion, but, as Bury says, 'there was one at least who did not waver in his faith that the movement was a giant's step on the path of man towards ultimate felicity, however far he had still to travel'.[2] This was Condorcet, Girondin, Encyclopaedist, friend and biographer of Turgot and Voltaire, who wrote his *Sketch of a Historical Picture of the Progress of the Human Spirit* in

[1] *De la félicité publique*, First Edition, Vol. II, p. 55.
[2] Op. cit., p. 206.

1793, as in the months preceding his tragic death he lay in hiding from Robespierre. The past history of humanity is here regarded as a continuous and uninterrupted progress, beginning with barbarism in which man is distinguished from the brutes only by his better bodily organization, and ending with the crisis of 1789. It is divided into nine stages each of which is marked by a definite advance in knowledge and enlightenment. From this survey Condorcet professes to derive his conviction of the inevitability of human progress throughout future time, unless some cosmic catastrophe should intervene. He then proceeds to a prophetic account of the tenth period, which he still valiantly believes is being inaugurated in his own time. The dominant notes are equality and perfectibility; equality both of nations and of classes; perfectibility alike of knowledge, virtue and bodily condition. Condorcet's is a very complete version of the eighteenth-century doctrine of progress, as it was worked out in France.

§ 22

Though the ideas whose history we have been tracing are preponderantly French in origin, very little delay attended their reflection in British thought. The note of secular optimism soon became as characteristic of the one country as of the other. As regards the earlier period the main difference is that the English thinkers were much less inclined to associate their hope of progress with political action. England was already in possession of free political institutions such as were the envy of France, and it consequently tended to limit the function of the state to the mere preservation of such orderly conditions as would enable men to work out their own progress within it, whereas the French thinkers counted largely upon the action of the state itself for the realization of their dreams. This is the essential difference between liberalism and socialism, both of which are equally progressive, but each of which has its own distinctive view of the process by which progress is to be achieved. However, as the eighteenth century drew towards its close, a more revolutionary note began to be heard in England also. It is already audible in Richard Price's *Observations on Civil Liberty* in 1776—the pamphlet which so much influenced the American Revolution.[1] It is trumpeted in Thomas Paine's *The Rights of Man* in 1791. It is sounded no less clearly in the anarchism of Godwin's *Enquiry Concerning Political Justice* in 1793; while socialism makes its first definite appearance in the life and work of Robert Owen after the turn of the century.

It is, however, significant that from the beginning the prevailing tendency in Britain was to regard the belief in earthly progress, not as an alternative to the traditional Christian outlook, but as a supplement to it. There were indeed a few in England who followed the French lead by working out their ideas in deliberate opposition to the Churches, but there were many more who, being well

---

[1] For amusing reference to it see Kenneth Roberts's admirably racy novel, *Rabble in Arms*. The enthusiastic welcome given by Price to the French Revolution is severely condemned by Burke in his *Reflections*.

aware that their progressivism was in one of its aspects a derivative from Christian conceptions, sought rather to lead Christian thought itself in this new direction. Among the early votaries of progress Price and his friend Joseph Priestley were dissenting ministers, David Hartley was a loyal Anglican deterred from taking orders by some scruples about signing the Thirty-nine Articles, James Dunbar and Turnbull were professors of philosophy at Aberdeen, while Adam Ferguson acted as chaplain to the Black Watch before being appointed to his chair of philosophy at Edinburgh.[1]

§ 23

The influence of the new French ideas upon the German *Aufklärung* and Romantic Movement was in many respects even more profound than upon English thought; and here also, though little associated with orthodox churchmanship, these ideas were usually worked into as much as could be retained of the existing religious setting. Lessing's famous and influential brochure on *The Education of the Human Race* (1780) represented the Old and New Testament revelation as a progressive process of divine education by which God had led the human mind from a state of tutelage towards a final state of independent thought such as was only then beginning to emerge; but 'It will assuredly come! the time of a new eternal

[1] Owen was hostile to organized Christianity, but for the derivation of his ideas from earlier Christian sectaries see Ernst Troeltsch, *Die Soziallehren der christlichen Kirchen und Gruppen*, p. 824. (Troeltsch mistakenly calls him Richard Owen.)

Gospel, which is promised us in the Primer of the New Testament itself.'[1] Herder's *Ideas Towards a Philosophy of the History of Mankind*, published four years later, is written against a definite background of religious belief, though the progress of humanity is represented as a natural process in which God leaves man to work out his own salvation by the exercise of his own reason. Lessing and Herder between them are the real originators of the many nineteenth-century attempts, no small proportion of which continued to hail from Germany, to tell the story of world religion as a progressive development of human discovery culminating in the teaching of Jesus of Nazareth—though possibly destined to move on to yet greater heights.

In the same year that Herder published his *Ideas* Immanuel Kant published a short work entitled *Idea Towards a Universal History in a Cosmopolitan Interest*, which he followed eleven years later with his tractate *Towards Perpetual Peace*. In these writings he is clearly working with that progressive view of human affairs which had been made familiar by the French thinkers. But though he is optimistic about the future, he is cautiously so, and commits himself neither to any doctrine of inevitable progress nor to the formulation of any law by which it is guided. Moreover, he stands in contrast to the eudaemonism both of the French and of most of the English thinkers; to him the goal of human development is not the perfect happiness of mankind but its perfect obedience to the moral law—to which happiness can be added only by the trans-

[1] Op. cit., F. W. Robertson's translation, § 86.

cendent action of God. Yet, as his thought developed, he came to see clearly that humanity could as little hope, within the earthly period and under earthly conditions, to attain moral perfection as it could hope that with such perfect goodness perfect happiness would automatically be conjoined. His famous proof of the immortality of the soul in *The Critique of Practical Reason* (1788) gives clear evidence of this. His argument is that we are commanded to bring our wills into perfect conformity with the moral law, but that since such perfect conformity is beyond our reach, its place must be taken by a progress towards it *in infinitum*; if then it is unconditionally demanded of us that we should progress endlessly, an endless life must be granted to us in which such progress can take place.[1] This argument is of the greatest interest as showing how the idea of progress has now begun to change the conception not only of earthly but of heavenly life. The conception which here makes its first appearance came to exercise profound influence on nineteenth-century thought. All previous ages had regarded the heavenly life as a state of perfect possession, perfect rest and perfected holiness. It now came to be regarded by many rather as a prolongation of the earthly quest and task, so that after death men will resume their development from the point at which death had interrupted it. Kant's prognostications of earthly progress may be cautiously framed in comparison with those of a writer like Condorcet, but it is surely a signal triumph for the general idea of progress that it should thus have found

[1] Op. cit., *Dialectic*, II. 4.

its way through the gates of pearl into the City of Gold.

Kant himself was able to devote but a scantling of his philosophical labour to the problem of the interpretation of history, but it was otherwise with his successors of the German idealist movement. For Fichte, Schelling and Hegel the philosophy of history was a main concern, and each was anxious to construe the course of events as following a forward-moving pattern. But what strikes us at once about these German writers is that they no longer pretend to base this reading of history upon a merely empirical foundation. They all work with the maxim that *das Historische dient nicht zur Demonstration, sondern nur zur Illustration*—that history does not demonstrate but merely illustrates. The observed course of events in any particular field—whether of political institutions, religious ideas, aesthetic taste or what not—illustrates and exemplifies the ideal pattern while at the same time confirming the cor-rectness of our understanding of it, but the pattern itself is given in the very nature of that reason which is the source and ground of all being. It is therefore discoverable by logical analysis. Of course it could not be known by us prior to all experience, but any bit of experience will reveal it as the *a priori* ground of its own possibility and as the pattern of its own internal structure, so that when we pass from the analysis of this bit of experience to that of any other, we shall know what to expect. We cannot indeed anticipate the concrete richness of the logical structure of any field of experience until we proceed to the empirical investigation of it, since only very slowly does the reason that is in us move towards a full consciousness of its own nature. Nevertheless the structure of all experience is given *a priori* in the nature of Absolute Spirit, and the clue to the nature of the whole is implicit in each separate part.

Such a summary statement covers ground that is common to all these idealist thinkers, though it does not follow the precise formulation of any one of them. Each of them offers us a reading of the past in the light of an *a priori* structure of experience as revealed to logical analysis. To Fichte's account of the successive stages of human history Schelling adds an account of organic growth, while Hegel offers an elaborate separate treatment of the different strands of human experience, such as religion, art and law.

We cannot but be aware, however, that with this thought of history as following an *a priori* logical pattern we have passed on to ground very different from that occupied by the French *philosophes* and the eighteenth century in general. Where we had formerly heard of progress we now hear rather of *development*. To the modern ear the two terms sound very much alike, since, as we shall see, the tendency of the later nineteenth century was to fuse them into one. Yet there is good reason for regarding them as in origin largely independent of one another. The idea of progress, as we have studied it from Bacon and Descartes onwards, was oriented towards the future. It was only occasionally, and mainly in such late writers as Condorcet, that the past was subjected to a progressive pattern, the prevailing tendency being rather to denigrate the past and to believe that from now on-

wards—or perhaps from as far back as the Renaissance—
progress was assured. On the other hand, the idea of development is applied mainly to the interpretation of past
history, and some of its principal advocates seem not at
all interested in future progress.

Development means unfolding, and the application of
this concept to history implies that later historical experiences are in some way an unfolding of what was latently
contained in earlier experiences of the same series. This
kind of continuity in history was not at all implied in the
idea of progress, the purposes of which would be sufficiently served by regarding history as a chain of entirely
discrete experiences, so long as only each new one was
better than the last. The case of Giambattista Vico is in-
structive in this regard. There is in his work something
like anticipation of the German idea of development, yet
hardly an idea of progress. Vico died in 1744, but it was
not until the German idealist and romantic movement
was well under way that his influence made itself widely
felt; a selection of his writings being translated into French
by the historian Michelet in 1835. Like Hegel, Vico interpreted history in terms of a logical (or perhaps in his case
rather more psychological) pattern inherent in the human
mind, and like Hegel he believed that this inherent structure of the human mind was ultimately grounded in the
mind of God. He therefore held that the natural unfolding
of human mentality caused every society to pass, in respect of all its institutions, through a cycle of three stages;
and in this way he was able to construct his 'eternal ideal
history, or course of humanity, followed by all nations'.

Professor Collingwood contends that 'Vico's cyclical movement is not a mere rotation of history through a cycle of fixed phases; it is not a circle but a spiral; for history never repeats itself, but comes round to each new phase in a form differentiated from what has gone before.'[1] Benedetto Croce, who has studied Vico to better effect than any other modern writer, hardly seems to agree. 'Vico,' he writes, 'who allowed no other reality in the republic of men than their history developing in an eternal spiritual rotation from feeling to intellect, from force to morality, yet materialized his ideal circle so that history lost the individuality of its actions with him. . . . Historiography with him lost its colour and turned to a static sociology, and the concept of progress and the unity of historical development failed him.'[2] 'Vico', he says again, 'allowed himself to be oppressed by the idea of "course" and "recourse" as a law of nature imposed upon

[1] *The Idea of History* (1936), p. 67 f.

[2] *History as the Story of Liberty* (English translation 1941), p. 78 f. We may quote the following from the (unsigned) article on Vico in the Eleventh Edition of the *Encyclopaedia Britannica*: 'It has been justly observed by many that this continuous cyclical movement entirely excludes the progress of humanity towards a better future. It has been replied that these cycles are similar without being identical, and that, if one might differ from another, the idea of progress was not necessarily excluded by the law of cycles. Vico undoubtedly considered the poetic wisdom of the Middle Ages to be different from that of the Greeks and Romans, and Christianity to be very superior to the pagan religion. But he never investigated the question whether, since there is a law of progressive evolution in the history of different nations, separately examined, there may not likewise be another law ruling the general history of these nations, every one of which must have represented a new period, as it were, in the history of humanity at large. Therefore, although the *Scienza nuova* cannot be said absolutely to deny the law of progress, it must be allowed that Vico not only failed to solve the problem but even shrank from attacking it.'

history; . . . and thereby he shut himself off from the idea of progress.'[1] The truth of the matter appears to be that Vico does really anticipate something of the later idea of spiral development which issues in genuine novelty, but is without the conviction that the new is better than the old, and therefore without the idea of progress.

Indeed even of the German idealists it must be said that they are almost more concerned to exhibit history in terms of immanental development, making each successive stage the logically necessary unfolding of something that was already contained in the matrix of the preceding one, than they are to establish the point that this development is in the direction of greater good. Furthermore, in the case of Hegel, we are left to the end in some doubt as to how far the *chronological* order of events is bound to follow the *logical* order of development which is confessedly his main concern. It would seem that, recognizing the interference of the element of historical contingency, he holds the rational order to be only partly reflected in the actual sequence of events. At the same time we must remember that he uses the rational order, not merely for the construction of a system of pure logic, but for his treatment of history itself; the contingent, he would say, is in itself meaningless and does not lend itself to historical treatment in any significant sense of the word. Moreover, he does quite certainly regard the Western, and particularly the Germanic, institutions of his own post-Napoleonic time as marking the culmination of a development which must

---

[1] Op. cit., p. 82.

therefore have been to that extent chronologically progressive.[1]

It is Croce, whose own philosophy of history owes much to the influence of Hegel and has the idea of development for its central principle, that has most strongly insisted on the mutual independence of the ideas of development and progress. Of the period from Descartes to the French Revolution he writes:

'The progress so much discussed was, so to speak, a progress without *development*, manifesting itself chiefly in a sigh of satisfaction and security, as of one favoured by fortune who has successfully encountered many obstacles and now looks serenely upon the present, secure as to the future, with mind averted from the past, or returning to it now and then for a brief moment only, in order to lament its ugliness, to despise or to smile at it.'[2]

But the conception of development, which, after its early anticipation by Vico, came to dominate the German idealist thought of the Romantic period from Lessing and Herder to Hegel, makes history the unfolding of 'ideal values'.[3]

'The whole of history is now understood as necessary development, and is therefore implicitly, and more or less explicitly, all

[1] Collingwood writes that for Hegel 'since all history is the history of thought and exhibits the self-development of reason, the historical process is at bottom a logical process. Historical transitions are, so to speak, logical transitions set out on a time-scale. History is nothing but a kind of logic where the relation of logical priority and posteriority is not so much replaced as enriched or consolidated by becoming a relation of temporal priority and posteriority. Hence the developments that take place in history are never accidental, they are necessary; and our knowledge of an historical process is not merely empirical: it is *a priori*, we can *see* the necessity of it.'— *The Idea of History*, p. 117.

[2] *Theory and History of Historiography* (English translation, 1921), p. 244.
[3] Ibid., p. 272.

redeemed; it is all learned with the feeling that it is sacred, a feeling reserved in the Middle Ages for those parts of it only which represented the opposition of God to the power of the devil.'[1]

Development thus implies the rejection of the notion that there is a transcendent unchanging reality behind or beyond the historical process, and makes that process itself the only reality there is. There is no permanency without change and no change without permanency, but only a process in which that which abides is nevertheless subject to change; 'for development is a perpetual surpassing, which is at the same time a perpetual conservation'.[2] Such is Croce's explication of the new-emerging idea.[3]

The absence from Hegel's pages of any particular outlook on the future is certainly remarkable. Whereas the French and English thinkers had at most interested themselves in past progress as disclosing an upward tendency which could be counted upon to continue itself far beyond the very unsatisfactory point which it had now reached, Hegel gives the impression of being content with what has already been achieved. The logical self-development of finite spirit is, he would almost seem to say, completed with the appearance of the Prussian monarchical state, while Absolute Spirit achieves in the Hegelian philosophy a final understanding of its own nature. Something of the Hegelian dialectic was later on incorporated by others into their own philosophy of reform and revolution. Hegel himself, however, had no interest in reform but only in philosophy; and the task of philosophy, as he

[1] Ibid., p. 270.   [2] Ibid., p. 84.
[3] Cf. also the illuminating essay of Dr. E. W. Lyman in *The Kingdom of God and History* (Church, Community and State Series, 1938), p. 73 ff.

conceived it, was to bring to full self-consciousness the movement of spirit which had already been accomplished. In the preface to his *Philosophy of Right* he wrote:

'Regarding the attempt to teach the world what it ought to be, we need only say that philosophy at least always comes too late for this. Philosophy is the thought of the world, and makes its first appearance only after reality has completed its process of formation. . . . When philosophy paints in grey on grey, one form of life has already become old, and by means of this grey on grey it cannot be rejuvenated but only known. The owl of Minerva begins its flight only as the dusk approaches.'

His work, then, as he conceived it, was not to forecast the future or even to influence it, but to interpret the past. Nevertheless his neglect of the further prospect cannot be attributed solely to this limited view of his own calling; for there is in it also a very evident strain of complacency in respect both of the finality of his own teaching and of the satisfactoriness of the condition of humanity in his time.

It will, however, be realized from what has been said that the thought of Hegel marks another new beginning. The progress of which the French and English thinkers spoke was but a phenomenon of human history on the surface of this planet, whereas Hegel carries up his notion of development into the ultimate nature of things.[1] This,

---

[1] Something of the sort is already present in the earlier thought of Fichte, though it disappears from his later writings which teach that God or the Absolute 'does not enter into process'. See Pringle-Pattison, *Hegelianism and Personality* (1887), p. 77: 'But it is at least apparent that he [Fichte] now ascribes to God an existence out of and beyond the process of evolution which formerly constituted his entire universe.' As for Schelling, Alfred Weber writes in his *History of Philosophy*, English translation, p. 498: 'In Schelling things proceed from the absolute, which for that very reason remains outside of them. In Hegel, *the absolute is the process itself.*'

too, is a consequence of his derivation of the laws of development, not from the particular psychological constitution of human nature, but from the nature of universal reason. No doubt he might have contented himself with saying that, though the process of events in time is controlled by the logical pattern of ultimate reality, yet that pattern itself subsists in the unchanging completeness of Absolute Spirit. Sometimes this does seem to be his meaning, and yet it is for him almost impossible of statement, since the traditional distinction of created from uncreated being finds no place whatever in his system, its place being taken by the distinction between finite and infinite being. Accordingly he is often found using language which implies that Absolute Spirit, which to him is alone ultimate reality, realizes itself only in the chronological process of history, and first reaches complete self-consciousness of its own nature in that logical understanding of the historical process which Hegel believed himself to have achieved. As it is put by Pringle-Pattison:

'It is the Absolute itself which arrives at full self-consciousness in the absolute philosophy. The Absolute is this process and its culmination. And it will be noted that just as this view of the Absolute comes into prominence, the other view of it as existing timelessly in static perfection recedes into the background, and becomes unreal. It is, however, the very heart and gist of the Hegelian philosophy that these two are one. The Absolute of the system is professedly a reconciliation of the divine and the human, the infinite and the finite, aspects of existence; and in order to achieve this unity Hegel is bound to represent the subject of the development and the perfect subject which forms the presupposition of the whole development as one and the same subject. He turns round, therefore, to assure us that what thus appears under the form of time exists really in an eternal present.'[1]

Thus the idea of progressive development, which in Kant had already found its way through the gates of pearl into the everlasting life of the saints, begins with Hegel to enter into the very life of God. Development is no longer conceived as occurring merely *within* reality. Reality is itself developing. This view, as we shall see presently, was destined to reappear in a much more confidently explicit form in the twentieth-century systems of William James, Samuel Alexander, Professor Whitehead —and Benedetto Croce.

Finally, it must be noted that whereas the earlier faith in progress was fundamentally libertarian, having as its basis a firm confidence in man's will to use his advancing knowledge in the service of the highest ends, the Hegelian notion of development is as fundamentally determinist, being grounded in logical necessity. This is the source of the uncertainty, noted at the beginning of the chapter as troubling the minds of contemporary votaries of progress, whether such progress is or is not to be regarded as inevitable.

§ 24

The German movement which we have thus briefly summarized from Lessing to Hegel was destined to exercise a very profound influence upon the Western thought of the nineteenth century. From now onwards not only the philosophy of history but the practice of historio-

[1] *Hegelianism and Personality*, p. 189.

graphy was to be dominated by this notion of development, that is, by the idea that each new historical emergent is an unfolding of something which was already latent in the womb of the preceding one. The historian was thus provided with a clue which enabled him to find his way through the infinite welter of his raw material, to discriminate between the significant and the merely trivial facts, and so to bring some sort of order into the arrangement of the whole. The effect was on the one hand enormously to stimulate historical research into every strand of human experience, and on the other to make it very difficult for anybody to write the history of anything without exhibiting it as a progressive development 'from the earliest times to the present day'.

In another way also those thinkers of the German Enlightenment and Romantic Movement were afterwards found to have stimulated thought in two very different and ultimately contrary directions. They were all friendly to Christianity, representing it as the culmination of the development of at least the religious thought of the race, but this soon resulted in a reciprocal friendliness of Christian thought towards the idea of development for which they stood. On the one hand theologians began to replace the traditional Christian reading of the *past* by a new reading of it in terms of continuous immanental development rather than of abruptly separated and transcendentally determined 'dispensations'. Pagan religion and culture were no longer regarded as a trackless jungle of devilish error, but as a steadily advancing quest of the true light; nor was the Bible itself any longer regarded as being on the same level of truth and significance in all its parts, but rather as a record of slowly developing insight which reached its culmination in the teaching of Jesus Christ. On the other hand the hope of *future* progress was widely adopted into Christian thought—as the result of a now general fusion of the notion of development with the earlier notions of progress; such usually being conceived as a gradually increasing conformity of individual and social morality to the New Testament teaching, though occasionally it came to be conceived also as an advance of moral and spiritual insight beyond the New Testament level.

It may perhaps be said that Lessing had most to do with the changed outlook on the future, and Hegel with the changed outlook on the past. But the fact that all these German thinkers, though friendly to Christianity, made so free with the traditional understanding of it and rather fitted it (or as much of it as they could) into the framework of their own independent outlook than conformed their outlook to its requirements, encouraged certain others to detach the same general body of ideas as far as possible from the Christian faith, and even to use it as a platform from which the Christian faith might be attacked. Of the influence of Hegel this is especially true. 'Hegel's religious philosophy', it has been said, 'was from the first a *Janus bifrons*, from which accordingly the theology to which it gave birth was developed in two contrary directions.'[1] The Right Wing of Hegelianism produced theologians

[1] Otto Pfleiderer, *The Development of Theology in Germany Since Kant*, English translation, p. 131.

like Marheineke and Daub in Germany, and at a later date theologians (of a more mediating temper, it is true) like John Caird in Great Britain; while the Left Wing has produced radical thinkers of the type of Feuerbach, David Friedrich Strauss and—greatest portent of all—Karl Marx.

The Marxist version of the Hegelian dialectic illustrates very well two of the paradoxes which we noted at the beginning of this chapter as having attended the movement of progressivist thought. Hardly more than Hegel does Marx concern himself with the continuation of progress throughout an indefinite future. Like Hegel his thought stops short with a proximate realization, the difference being that while the conservative Hegel is content with a political condition already reached, the revolutionary Marx projects his thought as far as the appearance of a classless society beyond the coming class war and proletarian revolution. Secondly, Marxist thought is haunted by the antinomy between inevitable progress and human free will. The relation of human freedom to divine predestination had of course long been a problem for Christian theology, but the difficulty of the problem is greatly aggravated when on the one hand logical necessity is substituted for divine purpose, and on the other hand human freedom is summoned to work out its own salvation by revolutionary means. Here it will be enough to quote a single passage in which Frederick Engels attempts a solution of the difficulty:

'History is so made that the end result always arises out of the conflict of many individual wills in which every will is itself the product of a host of special conditions of life. Consequently there

exist innumerable intersecting forces, an infinite group of parallelo-
grams of forces which give rise to one resulting product—the historical event. This again may itself be viewed as the product of a
force acting as a Whole without consciousness or volition. For what
every individual wills separately is frustrated by what everyone else
wills, and the general upshot is something which no one willed. And
so the course of history has run along like a natural process; it also
is subject essentially to the same laws of motion. But from the fact
that the wills of individuals—who desire what the constitution of
their body as well as external circumstances, in the last instance
economic (either personal or social), determine them to desire—do
not get what they wish but are sunk into an average or common
result, from all that one has no right to conclude that they equal
zero. On the contrary, every will contributes to the result and is in
so far forth included within it.'[1]

The German thinkers, as we have seen, had derived
much of their inspiration from earlier French thought,
but they were now in considerable measure to repay the
debt, their speculations exercising a profound influence
on the France of the post-revolutionary period. Yet the
French historians and historian-philosophers of this period
made their own very independent use of the German ideas
and it is probably to them—especially to the writings of
Victor Cousin and F. P. G. Guizot—that we owe, more
than to any others, the astonishingly complete naturaliza-
tion of the notion of developmental progress within
nineteenth-century thought. Moreover it was in France
that the headiest of all the vintages of the new wine were
now to be brewed. The systems of Fourier, Saint-Simon
and Comte all take their rise in the notion of progress, and

[1] Letter to J. Bloch, 21 September 1890. English translation in Appendix
to Sidney Hook's *Towards the Understanding of Karl Marx* (1933).

each is directed towards social and cultural reform of the most radical kind. Nevertheless, though all are inimical to institutional Christianity, each decks itself out in a religious dress which contains many elements borrowed from the Christian tradition, and each leads to the foundation of a new sect. It is also important to notice from what strains of the Christian tradition these borrowings were made. Mr. Christopher Dawson writes:

'The older philosophic theory of progress, with its dogmatic appeal to Reason, and its reliance on the authority of an enlightened despotism, corresponds to the Christian tradition in its orthodox form, while the doctrine of the revolutionary idealists has an even closer affinity with the apocalyptic hopes of the earlier Millennarians and Anabaptists. Indeed it is often difficult to distinguish the descriptions of the social millennium of the revolutionaries from those of a purely religious apocalyptic. . . . This millenniarist conception of progress is specially characteristic of the early Socialists. It reached its climax in Fourier, whose speculations surpass in extravagance the wildest dreams of Cerinthus and his followers.'[1]

Thus, as was already noted at the beginning of this chapter, the idea of progress inclines to assume a new form with the emergence of socialist thought. The hope of a slow upward movement throughout a future indefinitely continued gives place to the lively expectation of a new order which can be brought about almost at a stroke by radical social rearrangement and which will then require no further important change. But the general idea of progress has now acquired so firm a hold on Western thought that few minds remain unaffected by it. It leads the revolutionary socialist to dream of a 'brave new world' just

[1] *Progress and Religion*, p. 197.

135

round the next turning; it encourages the liberal thinker to look forward to a slow but steady advance; while even conservative thinkers, though remaining sceptical of the possibility of improving the existing social structure, begin to believe that the future is likely to reveal a progressive improvement both of individual morality on the one hand and of material prosperity on the other.

Hegel and Comte are the two nineteenth-century thinkers who have supplied history with the most elaborately wrought progressive patterns. Their patterns, however, were not only very different in themselves but were supplied for very different purposes. Hegel's interest in the past was that only through an understanding of its movement could he grasp the eternal nature of reality, while Comte's interest was that it provided him with such laws of historical movement as enabled him at the same time to predict and to influence the future. Hegel writes as if he were standing at the end of historical development, whereas Comte writes as if he himself were preparing the way for its most significant period. His division of history into three states or stages is well known: the Theological stage, when events were explained by reference to personal divine powers, and which came to an end with the Renaissance; the Metaphysical stage, now coming to an end, when they were explained by reference to abstract depersonalized entities; and the Positive stage, now being inaugurated, when they will be explained by reference to invariable natural laws empirically discovered. At the root of his system lies the belief that the sequence of human thought and behaviour is as much subject to invariable law as the course of external nature, and it is this law which he believes himself to have discovered in his elaboration of the three stages, thereby making possible for the first time a genuine science of society. His first object of research, he tells us, was 'to discover and demonstrate the laws of progress, and to exhibit in one unbroken sequence the collective destinies of mankind, till then invariably regarded as a series of events wholly beyond the reach of explanation, and almost depending on arbitrary will'.[1] Not only does the possession of such a science of society enable us to predict the future development of the race in the same way that physical science enables us to predict future happenings in external nature, but it also enables us to control the human future as physical science enables us to control the external world. The society of the future will be organized in accordance with the newly discovered sociological laws. This, however, cannot be done without a profound development of the moral feelings in the direction of a general altruism, nor can any such development be expected except under the inspiration of religion. Comte therefore has no alternative but to found a new religion, and this he sets about to do with the greatest possible zeal, providing it with all possible trappings (for they could be no more) of priestly hierarchy, worship, ritual, symbol and dogma, in re-adaptation of the Christian system. Yet, since God must be dispensed with, the object of worship —le Grand Être—can only be Humanity itself; and since

[1] *Positive Polity*, Vol. III; quoted and reference given in *Encyclopaedia Britannica*, 11th Edition, article 'Comte'.

Christ too must be dispensed with, a new Trinity must be discovered within the same humanist limits. Comte's system is pure secularism in the strict and only true sense of the term, and the task he sets himself is the apparently self-contradictory one of inventing a secularist religion. The result was described by one witty observer as 'Catholicism *minus* Christianity'.

Nevertheless Comte's influence upon later thought, if somewhat diffuse, has been very far-reaching. Nowhere was it greater than among the rationalist thinkers of later nineteenth-century England, though most of these did their best to forget the fantastic top-dressing of cultus. 'Auguste Comte', writes Bury, 'did more than any preceding thinker to establish the idea of progress as a luminary which could not escape men's vision.'[1]

§ 25

Although Comte began the publication of his *Cours de philosophie positive* in 1830, it was not (with some few exceptions) until after the middle of the century that his ideas began to be absorbed into the thought of the English rationalists. Then, in 1859, Darwin published his *Origin of Species*.

It is sometimes unreflectingly supposed by those who have not stayed to discover the facts that the modern idea of progress originated as an extension of the doctrine of organic evolution. Actually the reverse is nearer the truth. The nineteenth-century discoveries in the biological field

[1] Op. cit., p. 290.

were themselves stimulated by the prior existence in the minds of the earliest investigators of the ideas of development characteristic of German romanticism but reaching them indirectly through the mediation of the Comtian positivists. Evolution and development are in themselves synonymous terms; they both mean unfolding; and the German word *Entwicklung* covers both. But in English at least the word evolution has come to be so closely associated with the new conceptions introduced by the biologists that it will here be convenient to reserve it for that use, continuing to employ the terms development and progress where wider senses are intended. At the same time we shall see that the new conceptions, when they appeared, resulted in an immense reinforcement of the tendencies which had been a precondition of their own appearance, seeming to provide them with a more solid foundation than any hitherto suggested.

Evolution, as Darwin was concerned with it, is a narrowly biological doctrine, having to do only with mutations in the structure of living organisms on the surface of this planet. Ordinary experience everywhere suggests the fixity of specific structures, and the testimony of such experience had traditionally been taken at its face value. The immutability of species is not a Christian doctrine any more than is the conception of a geocentric universe; both were in earlier ages common to Christians and non-Christians, forming part of the accepted scientific or common-sense world-view of those ages. Even Hegel, who had carried the idea of development further than any previous thinker, had refused to apply it to the organic realm, insisting that nature and history are two entirely different things, that nature has no histories, and that natural species, though exhibiting a logical hierarchy, are temporally immutable. Nevertheless, there had already been not a few suggestions to the contrary. Something of the kind had already appeared in Anaximander, Empedocles and (above all) in Epicurus in ancient Greece, and had been reflected in Lucretius's epic. And in the early nineteenth century the scientific mind was beginning to be open to the possibility that species, instead of being fixed, were subject to a process of development from the simpler to the more complex. The significance of Darwin lies partly in the fact that he brought forward new evidence of such development as well as codifying existing evidence more completely than anyone had done before him; but chiefly in the fact that he hit upon a means whereby such development may take place—or indeed *must* take place, since the said means (the survival of the fittest in the struggle for existence) was known to be in operation.

The only progress promised us through the operation of this principle of Natural Selection is the progressive replacement of those forms of organic life which are less able to cope with a given natural environment by such forms, appearing in the first place as fortuitous variations of established kinds, as are better able to cope with it.[1]

[1] 'Natural selection is a negative factor; it can account for the non-survival of those forms which have died out. Its work of elimination can be seen in operation in neglected gardens or waste land anywhere. There is nothing directional about it. The way it works depends on circumstances. If the climate changes from wet to dry, characters that were a handicap in the wet climate become an asset, and vice versa.'—A. D. Ritchie, *Civilization, Science and Religion* (1945), p. 139 f.

Such progress, however, could not in itself offer any encouragement to the contemporary optimism regarding the future of human society. Before that could be, it would have to be shown, first, that the further mental development of the human species continued to be controlled by the same laws as had led to the emergence of the species itself, and second, that a development so controlled is likely to lead us in the direction either of greater virtue or of greater felicity.

The more cautious exponents of the doctrine of evolution were often careful to warn us against finding in it a foundation for any such optimism. Most famous is the warning sounded by Huxley in his Romanes Lecture. The cosmic process which controls the formation of species bears, he argued, no relation whatever to moral ends, and 'the imitation of it by man is inconsistent with the first principles of ethics'. Human altruism must ever stand firmly opposed to the selfish struggle for existence which is the law of the vegetable and animal kingdoms. At the same time, and in the same context, Huxley reminded us that even the course of organic evolution is certain one day to turn back upon itself:

'That which lies before the human race is a constant struggle to maintain and improve, in opposition to the State of Nature, the State of Art of an organized polity; in which, and by which, man may develop a worthy civilization, capable of maintaining and constantly improving itself, until the evolution of our globe shall have entered so far upon its downward course that the cosmic process resumes its sway; and, once more, the State of Nature prevails over the surface of our planet.'

Therefore,

'the theory of evolution encourages no millennial expectations. If, for millions of years, our globe has taken the upward road, yet, some time, the summit will be reached and the downward route will be commenced. The most daring imagination will hardly venture upon the suggestion that the power and the intelligence of man can ever arrest the procession of the great year.'[1]

Such warnings, however, had but a limited effect in deterring men from expanding the notion of evolution from the biological to the historical and ethical spheres, or from drawing from this extension further substantial encouragement for their hopes of progress. Huxley himself, as the passages just quoted are alone sufficient to show, entertained such hopes no less than the rest of his contemporaries, though on the one hand refusing to find confirmation for them in biological doctrine, and on the other hand clearly envisaging their final extinction with the degeneration of our solar system. (Incidentally it is interesting to remark in the last-quoted passage that this alternation of growth and decay connects itself in his mind with the ancient cyclical conception of the Great Year.) Nor was he even particularly averse from applying the name of evolution to this human progress, so long as only it be understood that its direction is in no sense a continuation of, but rather runs contrary to, the trend of the organic world. 'That progressive modification of civilization which passes by the name of the "evolution of society" is, in fact, a process of an essentially different

[1] *Evolution and Ethics* (Romanes Lecture for 1893), together with the Prolegomena to the same (1894); in Vol. IX of *Collected Essays*.

character from that which brings about the evolution of species. . . .'[1]

Moreover Huxley himself, for all his caution, encourages another extension of the conception of evolution which had already begun to lay hold on men's minds, namely its extension, not now forwards to the mental and moral realm, but backwards to the inorganic. Scientific discovery, he believes, is pointing to the belief that 'not merely living things, but the whole fabric of the earth; not merely our planet, but the whole solar system; not merely our star and its satellites, but the millions of similar bodies which bear witness to the order which pervades boundless space, and has endured through boundless time; are all working out their predestined courses of evolution.'[2] In both realms alike, inorganic as well as organic, evolution means a movement from uniformity to diversity, from simplicity to complexity of structure.

This pronouncement, however, is from the last years of Huxley's life, when it was already almost a commonplace, and is less boldly phrased than many similar ones. The notion grew apace that the whole course of temporal events constituted a single stream of tendency, governed by a single general law. Nor did the three apparent breaks seem incapable of being mortised. A more utilitarian ethic than Huxley's would conceal the break between organic and social development. The further study of anatomy and embryology, added to the discovery of earlier human types, suggested the one-time existence of a 'missing link' between the brute and human organisms.

[1] Op. cit., p. 37.   [2] Ibid., p. 7.

And finally the study of crystal formation and the behaviour of inorganic colloids on the one hand, and of the lowest forms of bacterial life (and finally of viruses) on the other, suggested the possible discovery of another 'missing link' between the organic and the inorganic. The audacious doctrine was thus not long in being mooted that the whole process of things from the 'primeval nebula' to the latest change in public opinion constitutes a single movement of evolutionary progress towards an eminently desirable goal.

The most influential exponent of a conception of evolution which thus covered alike the inorganic, organic and (as he called it) the 'super-organic' fields was Herbert Spencer who, stimulated thereto by Lyell's *Principles of Geology* and the researches in embryology of Karl Ernst von Baer,[1] had confidently adopted the evolutionary hypothesis even before Darwin had provided it with a causal explanation.[2] His *System of Synthetic Philosophy* attempted to embrace all the phenomena of the universe within the compass of a single general formula such as will cover all phases of that 'continuous transformation which the universe undergoes'. Of the inorganic development he has little to say in detail, though this defect was amply made good by later writers more learned in astronomy; but successive volumes dealt with the principles of biology, psychology, sociology and ethics, the last-mentioned dealing with those 'last stages in the evolution of conduct

[1] See R. C. K. Ensor, *Some Reflections on Herbert Spencer's Doctrine that Progress is Differentiation* (1946).
[2] Before the publication of Darwin's work he had followed the Lamarckian line, but after 1859 he changed over to that of Natural Selection.

. . . displayed by the highest type of being, when he is forced, by increase of numbers, to live more and more in presence of his fellows.' Spencer is more responsible than any other single writer for the tendency, so widely diffused in the closing decades of the century, to convert the doctrine of evolution into an instrument of unbridled optimism.

G. K. Chesterton once commented drily on the surprising number of people who *think* they have read *The Origin of Species*. And indeed it is surprising that Darwin's discovery of the principle which ensures the establishment of progressively fitter organic species, however revolutionary its effects in its own modest field of biological study, should thus have provided the foundation for an optimistic philosophy covering the whole cosmic process. In saying this, however, we must not forget that Darwin himself sounded an optimistic note in the penultimate paragraph of his book:

'We can so far take a prophetic glance into futurity as to foretell that it will be the common and widely spread species, belonging to the larger and dominant groups within each class, which will ultimately prevail and procreate new and dominant species. As all the living forms of life are the lineal descendants of those which lived long before the Cambrian epoch, we may feel certain that the ordinary succession by generation has never once been broken, and that no cataclysm has desolated the whole world. Hence we may look with some confidence to a secure future of great length. And as natural selection works solely for the good of each being, all corporeal and mental endowments will tend to progress towards perfection.'

§ 26

However, in the early years of the twentieth century the conception of evolution was destined to find a still bolder application. Spencer had embraced within its scope the whole sequence of temporal events, but behind that sequence, and sustaining it in being, he acknowledged the existence of an ultimate reality which he called the Unknowable. Now, however, it was to be suggested that the ultimate reality was itself subject to evolutionary progress, or, alternatively (though sometimes amounting to very much the same thing), that the temporal process which we familiarly know is all the reality there is. We have already noted a tendency in this direction in the Hegelian philosophy, or at least an ambiguity such as made it possible to read it in this sense. The historical process, it appeared, was a process in which the Absolute itself was achieving self-realization. But since Hegel regarded time as only a phenomenal form of eternity, the aspect of reality as eternally self-complete limited the significance of its aspect as process. It was here that the twentieth century grew bolder. Perhaps the process is itself the ultimate reality? Perhaps evolution is no mere happy rearrangement of elements within a constant sum of things entire, but the sum of things entire is itself evolving? Perhaps progress does not eventuate under the eyes, and by the prevenient and sustaining power, of a God who is eternally perfect and complete in Himself, but God too is progressing? An affirmative answer to these questions, or to some of them, was strongly suggested by Bergson's doctrine of 'Creative Evolution', however much he himself might protest that this went beyond his intention;[1] as also by William James's doctrine of a Finite God and His 'unfinished universe', and by his further teaching (as expressed in a famous passage) that 'God Himself . . . may draw vital strength and increase of very being from our fidelity' in the struggle to make a better world.[2] A little later such an answer was explicitly returned by some of the adherents of the doctrine of 'Emergent Evolution', especially by Samuel Alexander.

Starting from a belief in the essential interrelatedness of time and space, and from the consequent view that all individual existences are point-events, Alexander comes to regard space-time as the single primordial matrix out of which the whole process of the universe emerges. This process has a single definite direction towards the production of progressively higher values. The direction, however, is not, as Christianity has believed, given it by a transcendent God who is above the process, but is immanent in the process itself as a *nisus* or urge, which we may doubtless take as the equivalent of Bergson's *élan vital*. The course of evolution thus follows no preconceived plan, but works 'so as to produce a plan'. The plan is not yet finished, and never will be finished, since the process is in its very nature an unending one. 'There is a *nisus* in Space-Time which, as it has borne its creatures through matter and life to mind, will bear them forward

[1] Cf. A. S. Pringle-Pattison, *The Idea of God*, pp. 379–83.
[2] *The Will to Believe*, p. 61.

to some higher level of existence.'[1] And the level of existence next above that which has at any point emerged is what we mean by deity; so that for us at present God should mean 'the next higher empirical quality to mind, which the universe is engaged in bringing to birth'.[2] It is clear that on this view progress is no longer conceived as having place within, or against the background of, a more ultimate reality which is not itself subject to change. Reality itself is evolving. And God is neither the transcendent author of evolution nor even the immanent *nisus* that pushes it forwards. He is Himself a product of evolution, or rather one day will be. It is fundamental to the doctrine of Emergent Evolution to believe that each emergent level of existence is characterized by the introduction of genuine novelty. But if we ask where then the new quality comes from, since there is no reality outside the process from which it could proceed, Alexander replies that we must accept its appearance with what he calls 'natural piety', and ask no further questions. To which Dr. W. R. Matthews has replied: 'Almost any kind of piety is doubtless praiseworthy; but not the kind which forbids us to ask, Why? . . . We may suspect that "natural piety" is commended to us lest, pushing our questions beyond the appearances of things, we should be led to supernatural piety.'[3]

Lloyd Morgan, the other early exponent of this conception of emergence, does not however go so far. He too

---

[1] *Space, Time and Deity*, Vol. II, p. 346.
[2] Op. cit., p. 347.
[3] *God and Evolution* (1926), p. 40; a small book very well worth reading.

believes that 'not only atoms and molecules but organisms and minds are susceptible of treatment by scientific methods fundamentally of like kind; all belong to one tissue of events; all exemplify one foundational plan.'[1] But he differs from Alexander in holding that the emergent values are also in some sense 'ingredient'. To explain progress we must posit not only a *vis a tergo* acting from below, but also a *vis a fronte* acting from above.

'Without denying a felt push from the lower levels of one's being —a so-called driving force welling up from below—to me it feels like a drawing upwards through Activity existent at a higher level than that to which I have attained.'[2]

And this Activity is God; which means that something more than Alexander's 'natural piety' may be permitted us:

'A doctrine that acknowledges a direct Activity in evolution explains also from above, accepting, with its fitting form of piety, God who draws all things and all men upwards.'[3]

'What comes by nature is in my belief a Divine gift, manifested in others and revealed in oneself in the determinate advance of natural events. If I may so put it, emergent evolution is from first to last a revelation and a manifestation of that which I speak of as Divine Purpose.'[4]

Nevertheless we are left in some doubt as to the genuineness of the transcendence here accorded to God or to any reality beyond the process. The uncertainty we found in Hegel is felt again in such words as these:

[1] *Emergent Evolution* (1923), p. 2.
[2] Ibid., p. 208.
[3] Ibid., p. 62.
[4] *Life, Mind and Spirit* (1925), p. 145.

'The evolution of mind in the history of events is the progressive coming to its own, in the fulness of time, of the intelligence or reason inherent always in the very nature of the world. In the beginning the end was enfolded; but only through unfolding do we learn what was, from first to last, the nature of this enfolded end.'[1]

The speculative tradition whose course we have thus been sketching may be regarded as culminating in Professor Whitehead's Philosophy of Organism. Here the main concern is with the relation of process to reality; and *Process and Reality* is the name of his longest philosophical work, in the preface to which he expresses his great indebtedness 'to Bergson, William James and John Dewey'. Like these he rejects the traditional idea that process has its place only within, or against the background of, a timelessly perfect ultimate reality. He lays it down as a metaphysical principle that 'the very essence of real actuality—that is, of the completely real—is *process*'.[2] 'The process is itself the actuality, and requires no antecedent static cabinet.'[3] 'Thus a process must be inherent in God's nature, whereby his infinity is acquiring realization.'[4] That last is very reminiscent of Hegel, and indeed we are constantly being reminded of Hegel in the reading of Whitehead, in spite of a virtually complete absence of reference to him, and in spite also of Hegel's very different view of the relation of time to eternity. There is, we are told, 'a primordial nature of God', and 'a consequent nature of God' in which it issues. The rest had better be

[1] *Emergent Evolution*, p. 111.
[2] *Adventures of Ideas*, p. 354.
[3] Ibid., p. 356.
[4] Ibid., p. 357.

told in Professor Whitehead's own difficult but carefully chosen words:

'God is not to be treated as an exception to all metaphysical principles, invoked to save their collapse. He is their chief exemplification. Viewed as primordial he is the unlimited conceptual realization of the absolute wealth of potentiality. In this aspect, he is not *before* all creation, but *with* all creation. But, as primordial, so far is he from "eminent reality" that in his abstraction he is "deficiently actual".'[1]

'Thus when we . . . consider God in the abstraction of a primordial actuality, we must ascribe to him neither fulness of feeling nor consciousness.'[2]

'From this point of view, he is the principle of concretion—the principle whereby there is initiated a definite outcome from a situation otherwise riddled with ambiguity.'[3]

'But God, as well as being primordial, is also consequent. He is the beginning and the end. . . . Thus, by reason of the relativity of all things, there is a reaction of the world on God. The completion of God's nature into a fulness of physical feeling is derived from the objectification of the world in God. . . . But his derivative nature is consequent on the creative advance of the world. . . . The consequent nature of God is conscious; and it is the realization of the actual world in the unity of his nature and through the transformation of his wisdom.'[4]

Thus 'God is to be conceived as originated by conceptual experience, with his process of completion motivated by consequent, physical experience, initially derived from the temporal world.'[5]

We may remark that such a doctrine of the alone reality of process is best regarded as an extreme development of that side of the Hebrew outlook which is all but lacking from Greek philosophical thought, but to the total exclusion of that other element, in the Hebrew outlook,

[1] *Process and Reality*, p. 486.   [2] Ibid.
[3] Ibid., p. 448.   [4] Ibid.   [5] Ibid., p. 489.

namely the hidden transcendence of God, which has an affinity-in-difference with the dominant element in Greek thought, namely the alone reality of the supra-temporal.[1] It is also worth noting that Croce reaches a not dissimilar identification of process with reality, leading in his case to the explicit identification of history with philosophy, by direct descent from the German idealist conception of development, and without drawing at all on the conception of organic evolution.

On the other hand, as we now look back on the general movement of nineteenth-century thought, we cannot but be aware that the added confidence and scope given to the belief in progress by the discovery of organic evolution derived from an extension of the biological doctrine which was not justified by that doctrine itself but resulted from a combination, distilled under the influence of that doctrine, of the eighteenth-century confidence in progress and the German conception of immanental development. Here again, then, we have to do with *a priori* presuppo-

[1] The following words of Professor A. D. Ritchie are illuminating: 'The notion that the eternal or timeless is the sole, ultimate, and complete reality makes (or tends to make) the events of history no more than half real (for most Indian thought not real at all). That conclusion the Hebrews would have denied emphatically. So far as God is revealed at all, they held that He is revealed through His creation, the material world, and especially through the course of temporal events we call human history. . . . No Hellenic thinker considered the material world or the course of history in quite that light. . . . Plato, it is true, shows signs of hesitation and sometimes leans to a more Hebraic notion of the creativity of God and even of the reality of process. Still, there is generally a distinct cleavage of thought between the Hellenic view which takes historical process as a shadow-show, real only so far as it reflects eternal truth, and the Hebraic view that it is real in its own right as the direct working out of God's purpose, so that in some way time is necessary to eternity.'—*Civilization, Science and Religion* (1945), p. 53 f.

sition rather than with empirically ascertained fact. It is an alternative faith that is presented to us, not the displacement of faith by incontrovertible evidence. Whatever weight one may give to the progressive appearance of higher forms of organic life on the surface of this planet during a certain period of its existence, and however generous a meaning we may in this context give to the word 'higher', it can hardly be pretended that the extension of such evolutionary progress, from so strictly limited a field to the whole reality of things throughout infinite space and infinite time, is other than a highly speculative construction such as would be little likely to win acceptance from, and could perhaps not even have suggested itself to, minds not already, and through the operation of quite other influences, predisposed to its entertainment.

We have already seen, however, that the general idea of progress, while being developed by some in the direction of a naturalist or positivist outlook such as sought to displace the Christian faith, was at the same time employed by others in the service of that faith and with a view to what they conceived to be either a necessary revision or a further enrichment of it. It remains now only to note that this continued to be true of the evolutionary version of the doctrine. Just at first Christian thought reacted almost unanimously against the new ideas, finding itself unable to dissociate the fixity of species from the fundamental principles of the faith; nor has such opposition yet ceased to be represented among us. Within a very few years, however, many Christian thinkers began to come round to the view that the doctrine of evolution, instead of contradicting the essential Christian view of the divine ordering of the world, pointed the way to a greatly enriched and much more inspiring understanding of it. Henry Drummond's *Natural Law in the Spiritual World* (1883) and his *Ascent of Man* (1894), together with certain of the contributions to the *Lux Mundi* volume (1889), were early expositions of this point of view. Yet the most significant effect of evolutionary doctrine upon Christian theology was not the change that thus overtook Christian teaching about creation, but the encouragement it gave to the progressivist, which now came as frequently to be called the evolutionist, reading of history. And not least of sacred history, which was now to appear under the guise of the evolution of religion.

CHAPTER IV

THE AVAILABILITY OF THE PRESUPPOSITIONS

§ 27

OUR historical survey has gone far to confirm one significant impression borne in upon us at an earlier stage. In the first chapter we attempted to assess the kind and degree of progress of which men were empirically aware before they began to attach any particular importance to it or to find in the contemplation of it any particular spiritual support; and at the same time we ventured to enquire what further knowledge of progress was now available to us, on a like empirical basis, as the result of modern archaeological and historical research. Our finding was that the progress thus verifiable concerned chiefly such an understanding of our physical environment as led to an increased adjustment to it and consequent control over it, but extended also to such an understanding of our social environment as led to improved social techniques; whereas it barely reached the frontiers of the distinctively ethical and spiritual spheres. In the third chapter we traced the rise and growth of the philosophical or quasi-religious belief in progress, as a reality deep grounded in the nature of things to which men pinned their faith and which became for them a mainstay of confidence and hope. But here we found that the kind of progress chiefly occupying men's minds was progress in happiness, in wisdom, or in goodness. Not that the technical progress of humanity was now left out of account. Rather was more made of it than ever before; and in the later period the tale has been continued backwards from the specifically human to the general biological field, and even through the biological to the inorganic. But these lower stages of progress have been regarded as providing the necessary substructures for the emergence and development of the higher values, and it is on this latter that the emphasis has been placed.

We are therefore confirmed in the conclusion that the kind of progress which is certainly observable, and the kind imperatively required for the filling out of any kind of *a priori* faith in progress, barely overlap one another. To express it epigrammatically, observed progress is mainly technical, whereas believed progress is mainly spiritual. It thus becomes all-important to know whether we have any real ground for the assertion of an *a priori* principle which would lead us to look for spiritual progress in the past or expect it in the future. That must be our next problem; and following on it, we must enquire also whether such a belief in progress, even if substantiated, can really provide the spiritual satisfaction which men have sought from it.

§ 28

It will be convenient to begin with the latest proposed ground and work backwards, gradually peeling the onion of nineteenth-century confidence. We shall therefore first consider whether the idea of evolution provides the necessary principle. We need not challenge the truth of that idea within the strictly biological field to which alone it originally applied, but shall take that as granted for the purposes of argument. The question is only whether we have any real ground for extending the idea backward into the inorganic and forward into the historical fields, so turning it—as has been done—into some kind of cosmic principle.

The question of the backward extension is less important for us, because that alone would not materially alter the situation created by the acceptance of the biological doctrine. Whether this extension is legitimate depends on how much of the observed pattern of biological evolution we read into the meaning of the word evolution itself. If evolution means only that existing forms of being were not fixed at creation but have been generated out of earlier forms by a continuous process, then we may certainly speak of present astronomical doctrine as evolutionary in contrast to the earlier view that earth and sun and stars have always been as they are now. If we include also the idea that the direction of change is from simpler to more complex forms, there is probably still a sense in which we may describe the present nebular hypothesis as an evolutionary one. But if we further take up into our definition the ideas of increasing adjustment to environment by the survival of the fitter forms, then it becomes difficult to see how we can legitimately speak of the evolution of the sidereal universe. Moreover, when we turn from the macrocosmic field of astronomy to the microcosmic field of physical chemistry, the application of the conception of evolution is even more doubtful. It is true that elements formerly regarded as simple and therefore unchanging are now known to be composite and subject to change, and also that we know much about the processes by which simpler chemical forms may be transmuted into more complex and vice versa. But there seems no reason to suppose that the direction of change throughout past time has been from the simpler to the more complex. It is therefore difficult to know in what sense we could here speak of evolution. As a distinguished chemist has written:

'The idea of progressive development with time from the simple to the complex is really wholly foreign to the subject. In point of fact, as present knowledge goes, although we now know cases of the more complex elements spontaneously changing into the simpler, it still remains entirely hypothetical whether, as has been so often supposed, the reverse takes place in nature at all. . . . It is the merest obsession to extend such ideas to the inanimate world.'[1]

Passing then to the forward extension, we have to ask whether the concept of evolution can be usefully applied to the process of change characteristic of human culture. Here we do find (a) the development of later out of earlier forms, (b) a direction of change towards greater complexity of form, and (c) the control of such change by the need of adjustment to environment. So far there is analogy between the supposed course of organic evolution and the observed course of cultural history. We must, however, be careful to remember that we have found the above-mentioned characteristics to be applicable only to the technical, not to the spiritual, aspects of

[1] Professor Frederick Soddy in *Evolution in the Light of Modern Knowledge: A Collective Work* (1925), pp. 356, 402.

culture. Nor does any ground of an *a priori* kind appear for expecting that they should apply to the latter. Rather are there strong grounds to the contrary. It must be remembered that evolution, as known to biology, is essentially an unconscious and involuntary process. Even when the evolving subjects are conscious beings, the evolutionary result of their behaviour is not something they themselves have willed or foreseen. Had they foreseen it, they might not have liked it, and therefore might have willed the contrary and acted differently, preventing the realization of the evolutionary result. Hence, as soon as behaviour begins to be controlled by free intelligence, acting with a view to ideally conceived and freely chosen ends, the process of evolution is to that extent interfered with. Now all human behaviour is partly under the control of free intelligence, and partly also conditioned by the unconscious operation of natural factors, biological, geographic, economic and sociological; but it is obviously in regard to the most spiritual aspects of culture that intelligence has the freest play. Accordingly we need not be surprised that the changing forms of technical culture follow a direction which continues in some part the trend of vegetable and animal evolution, while the changing forms of spiritual culture cannot be observed to follow any such direction. But since even man's technical culture is always partly influenced by ethical ideals and religious ideas, as well as influencing these in turn, we should be on our guard against treating *any* aspect of historical change as a mere continuation of biological trends. It is on the whole safer to leave the term evolution to the biologists and to say that where change is determined by free intelligence, the evolutionary process is so far forth in abeyance. Professor Elliot Smith confirms us in this conclusion:

'In dealing with human beings who, in virtue of the acquisition of speech, are able to transmit information one to another and to hand on the fruits of experience to succeeding generations, a new state of affairs has arisen for which no exact parallel is found elsewhere. Hence the process involved in originating and diffusing knowledge and man's interpretation of it is something different from organic evolution. It is therefore dangerous and misleading to use such biological terms as "evolution" and "convergence", as many writers are now doing, in reference to cultural history and to circumstances that are fundamentally different from those biological phenomena in reference to which the terms in question were devised.'[1]

It is also well to remember that the kind of development to which the biologists give the name of evolution normally requires an unimaginable length of time in which to achieve even any considerable result, so that there can be little justification for seeking evidence of its operation within the span of human historical memory.[2]

Still less justified, however, if indeed not manifestly absurd, is the proposal to find in the doctrine of biological evolution support for the notion that ultimate reality is itself subject to evolutionary process. There is nothing whatever, and in the nature of the case there could be

[1] *Evolution in the Light of Modern Knowledge*, p. 315.
[2] 'Since the times of the Cro-Magnon race, probably twenty thousand years ago, there has been no marked increase in cranial capacity, and probably little or no increase in his [man's] inherent intellectual ability.'—Professor E. G. Conklin in *The Evolution of Earth and Man*, edited by G. A. Baitsell (1929), p. 395.

nothing whatever, in the recent discoveries of science that could even suggest such a notion. Common sense has always proceeded on the assumption that when novel elements appear in the course of any process of change, they must derive from some other quarter—something or Someone *else*—that is already real. Now, in such a philosophy as that of Alexander we are confronted with the alternative idea that they come from nowhere and Nobody (but just come), so that with their appearance the sum-total of reality is itself increased. It is difficult indeed to achieve the degree of 'natural piety' necessary to belief in miracles of this kind. Miracles were not altogether easy to believe, even when one also believed in the reality of a transcendent God to whose direct agency they might be attributed, but the situation becomes impossible when they cannot be attributed to any agency. *Creatio ex nihilo* was supposed to be a doctrine requiring faith for its acceptance even when it was held that the existence of a Creator could be established on purely rational grounds, but surely it calls not so much for faith as for credulity when the existence of a Creator is denied. It is worth while, even at the risk of repetition, to make sure that the reason of this is clearly grasped. Environment is necessary to evolution not only because the latter means nothing if not adjustment to environment, but for the much profounder reason that whatever increase an evolving being manifests must derive from its environment. Neither an organism nor anything else can grow in any other way than by taking up something into itself from that which surrounds it. Hence no being could grow if it were surrounded by nothing; hence reality as a whole cannot grow. This is what the Greeks saw so clearly and made the basis of their cosmology. Even Epicurus and Lucretius made it the basis of their cosmology and were consequently forced to the conclusion (odious to Alexander and his fellow 'Emergent Evolutionists') that no genuine novelty ever emerges in the course of evolution but only a redisposition of what was already there—the immutable atoms. This is indeed quite elementary, and nothing could be more certain. Only a false analogy has ever made anybody doubt it. The analogy is from the behaviour of organic life to that of universal being; and the analogy is false because organism presupposes environment, and universal being, by definition, can have no environment. Actually, however, it is clear that the adoption of their difficult new hypothesis by Professors Alexander, Dewey, Whitehead and others, in place of the traditional one, is based on some *a priori* preference concerning the origins of which they have done little to enlighten us, and not on anything suggested to them by the facts of biological evolution. Yet could there, after all, be a more flagrant case of anthropomorphism than that man should think to find in the sequence of changes occurring in the protoplasmic scum that forms a thin covering of the surface of this particular little planet—

> that small model of the barren earth
> Which serves as paste and cover to our bones—[1]

a law of change which controls the very life of God—or of whatever gods there be?

[1] Shakespeare, *King Richard II*, Act III, Scene II.

A further word must, however, be spoken concerning the relation of the idea of evolution to the idea of progress. The question is whether those processes which can with full propriety be described as evolutionary are found to exhibit a movement in a *desirable* direction towards a *good* end. Answering it in the affirmative Dr. Julian Huxley concludes that 'during the time of life's existence on this planet' there has been an increase in the size of organisms, in the duration of their life, in their complexity, in their integration, in their independence over against their environment, and in their psychical powers.

'This increase has not been universal; many organisms have remained stationary or have even regressed; many have shown increase in one particular but not in others. But the *upper level* of these properties of living matter has been continually raised, their average has continually increased. It is to this increase, continuous during evolutionary time, in the average and especially in the upper level of these properties that, I venture to think, the term biological progress can be properly applied.'[1]

The same conclusion, however, can probably be arrived at on grounds of a still more general kind. If it be true that an evolutionary process which began with protophytes and protozoa has resulted in the appearance of beings capable of spiritual life, the name of progress cannot be denied to it by those who hold spiritual to be the highest values. On the other hand, science offers us no ground for believing that such progress will continue throughout an indefinite future; on the contrary it invites us rather to believe that environmental changes will result

[1] *Essays of a Biologist* (1923), p. 31.

in eventual regress. Nor, as we have seen, does it warrant us in regarding the movement of human history, after free intelligence has begun to interfere with the operation of merely instinctive tendencies, as a continuation of the biological movement. It is in this sense true, as T. H. Huxley contended, that 'the cosmic process has no sort of relation to moral ends', and even that 'social progress means a checking of the cosmic process at every step and the substitution for it of another, which may be called the ethical process'.[1] We cannot therefore agree with his grandson, Dr. Julian Huxley, that a general belief in progress 'is clarified and put on a firm intellectual footing by biology'.[2]

§ 29

Continuing to peel the onion, we must next consider whether the principle of development, as present in earlier nineteenth-century thought before the superimposition of specifically evolutionary doctrine, provides a reliable *a priori* foundation for belief in progress.

---

[1] *Evolution and Ethics*, pp. 83, 81.

[2] *Essays of a Biologist*, p. 61. Dr. Julian Huxley continues: 'The problems of evil, of pain, of strife, of death, of insufficiency and imperfection—all these and a host of others remain to perplex and burden us. But the fact of progress emerging from pain and battle and imperfection—this is an intellectual prop which can support the distressed and questioning mind and be incorporated into the common theology of the future.' It is as true of scientists as of the rest of us that the reliability of their pronouncements is often in inverse ratio to (shall we say?) the square of the distance separating the object of their discourse from their own human interests.

Boswell thus reports Dr. Johnson:

'Great abilities are not requisite for an Historian; for in historical composition all the greatest powers of the human mind are quiescent. He has facts ready to his hand; so there is no exercise of invention. Imagination is not required in any high degree; only about as much as is used in the lower kinds of poetry. Some penetration, accuracy, and colouring will fit a man for the task, if he can give the application which is necessary.'[1]

This was the notion of history generally prevailing in the English empirical tradition of the seventeenth and eighteenth centuries, being grounded in the Baconian formula that the three spheres of human learning correspond to the three parts of the human understanding—philosophy to the reason, poetry to the imagination, and history to the memory. If an entirely different conception of the historian's task now prevails among us, the credit must largely go to the movement of German thought from Lessing to Hegel. We have all now come to see that the chaos of recorded fact is quite unmanageable apart from the presence of some guiding principle in the historian's mind, and that as Dr. Collingwood has written, 'the attempt to eliminate this "subjective element" from history is always insincere—it means keeping your own point of view while asking other people to give up theirs—and always unsuccessful. If it succeeded, history itself would vanish.'[2]

The guiding principle provided by the German idealists was the idea of development. With its aid the historian

[1] Boswell's *Life of Johnson*, Oxford edition, Vol. I, p. 284.
[2] *The Philosophy of History* (Historical Association Leaflet, No. 79, 1930), p. 15. Cf. also the note on page 25 above, and the quotation it contains from Professor Hodges.

was able to pick out the really significant facts from the welter of merely contingent happenings with which he was confronted. He was thus able to envisage the total past experience of the race as the progressive unfolding of a destiny which, though the promise of it was implicit in its earliest beginnings, could be understood only in the light of its final realization.

Now we have already ventured to affirm that there can be no true sense of history, and no significant historiography, which is not guided by some sense of a forward-moving pattern; and we have seen that the Hebrew-Christian tradition was the first to provide the human mind with such a pattern. The new pattern now suggested, though owing much of its inspiration to the earlier Christian one, is profoundly different in that it substitutes the unfolding of an immanent intelligence for the guidance of a transcendent Intelligence. But at least it provides history with a meaning, and the very fact that it is something of a new meaning gives fresh stimulus to the historical imagination. There is no doubt that both the debit and the credit, however these may be estimated, for the spectacular movement of historical studies throughout the nineteenth century, must in large part be set to the account of these German thinkers. The 'nineteenth century', writes Dr. Collingwood, 'saw an unparalleled development[1] of historical technique and historical knowledge; and this is closely associated with the gallant but unsuccessful attempt at universal "philosophical" history' of Vico, Herder and Hegel.[2]

[1] How the word will creep in!   [2] Ibid., p. 9.

An explicit statement of the view that there can be no significant history which is not a tale of progressive development is found in the little pamphlet on *The Presuppositions of Critical History* (1874) which was the earliest published work of the celebrated English idealist, F. H. Bradley. He assumes that history

'is a progress not only in the sense of that which increases in quantity, but in the sense of that which develops or evolves itself, is essentially the same in stages of growth which are diverse in quality, which differ from each other even more than the blossoms from the bud, and the fruit from the blossom.

'If the bud were self-conscious, it would know of itself, but not in the way that the blossom knows of it, still less as the fruit knows of it; and as failing of the truth, its knowledge must be said to be false. Still more is it so with history. In that ceaseless process which differentiates itself only as a means to integration, and which integrates itself only with the result of a fuller differentiation, the consciousness of the earlier stage of humanity is never the consciousness of a later development. The knowledge it has of itself is partial and false compared with the epoch of an intenser realization. . . . If the stages of evolution were essentially diverse, the possibility of history is inconceivable; and if history were a manifestation of human phenomena where all but the accidental was simply the same, the interest it excites would in no respect be higher than the pleasure we take in an ordinary novel.'[1]

Now of the various doctrines there contained the following seem to be common to Bradley's Hegelianism and the traditional Christian view: that some past events are charged with greater historical significance than others, that they have this significance because they are directional, that the direction in which they point is the ulti-

[1] Op. cit. as reprinted in Bradley's *Collected Essays* (1935), Vol. I, p. 39 f.

mate realization of a greater good, and that it is only in the light of this realization that their historical significance can be understood. Where the new view differs from the old one is that it puts the idea of the unfolding of the human spirit in accordance with its own immanent rational nature in place of the idea of a transcendent control whose action must be in large part unpredictable; and accordingly puts a universal gradualism in place of the recognition of discrete providential 'dispensations'. The purely immanental view of the relation of God to the world had long been present in Indian religion and philosophy and was already familiar to the modern West in the philosophy of Spinoza, but what is quite new in German romantic idealism is the combination of immanence with progress. For Indian thought history was an illusion; for Christian thought all history had a meaning, but this meaning was communicated to it through the medium of 'sacred history'; but what now happens is that the distinction between ordinary and sacred history is altogether dissolved, both being alike rewritten under the guidance of the notion of development. We have already quoted Croce's remark that in this new teaching (of which he himself is the most distinguished living advocate) 'the *whole* of history is . . . redeemed; it is *all* learned with the feeling that it is sacred'.[1] And in thus being redeemed, it apparently becomes itself redemptive; for in his later book Croce writes that 'the transcendental God is a stranger to human history, which would not exist if that God did exist; for History is its own

[1] See page 126 f. above; italics ours.

mystic Dionysus, its own suffering Christ, redeemer of sins'.[1]

It cannot but be remarked that the Christian view would seem to satisfy 'the presuppositions of critical history', which Bradley has in mind, quite as well as the new view which he himself adopts. Our question then is whether we have any reason to prefer the latter. It seems impossible to deny that the conception of immanental development has served to illuminate for us many tracts of history that formerly appeared both obscure and uninteresting. This is true of the history of pagan religion, but it is true also of our Christian 'sacred history'. To read any one of a long series of books that divides Cardinal Newman's *Essay on the Development of Christian Doctrine* from—choosing an example at random—Oesterley and Robinson's *Hebrew Religion, Its Origin and Development* is to find highly significant order in much that had otherwise been very confused. During the last hundred years the conception of development has become thoroughly domesticated in Christian historiography and has advantaged the latter greatly; so that we must in no wise be grudging in our acknowledgement of the debt now owed by Christian thought to Lessing, Herder and Hegel. Nor should there be any difficulty for the Christian in thus entertaining the conception of immanental development. It need imply no more than that God has dowered man with an understanding and conscience and spirituality of his own which moves from discovery to discovery by the propulsion of its own interior logic as well as under the

[1] *History as the Story of Liberty*, English translation, p. 30.

stimulus of unpredictable providential visitations. The Christian doctrine has always been that God is at the same time immanent and transcendent, indwells as well as overrules. It has never denied the reality of growth in grace and in insight, and has never, by denying all interior connexion between the stages of such growth, desired to interpret it solely as the result of a series of discontinuous divine actions. At the same time its recognition of such immanental development, and its understanding of its working, remained always on a strictly limited scale.

Thus while acknowledging gratefully the true insight contained in the new doctrine of development, and the enrichment it is capable of bringing to our Christian understanding of history when properly limited in its application, we can only regard it as having gravely misled us when it has been generalized, as by Hegel, into a universal formula. The facts of history simply will not be forced into such a mould, and there is no doubt that Hegel and his followers did great violence to them in the attempt so to force them. It would be unfair to say of Hegel himself, as was said of one of his followers, that 'facts bent like grass before his feet', for Hegel was after all no mean historian; but we may safely agree with Dr. Collingwood when he writes: 'The succession of historical periods is for Hegel a logical sequence of concepts, each concept the keynote of a period. Any idea of this kind is open to the fatal objection that it encourages the historian to plug the holes in his knowledge with something that is not history, because it has not been extracted from his sources.'[1] And

[1] *The Philosophy of History*, p. 8.

170

this is exactly what eventuated on so wide a scale. It is hardly possible to exaggerate the extent to which nineteenth-century, and especially late nineteenth-century, writing on the history of culture, of religion, of art and other things is now having to be scrapped and replaced, or at least rewritten, because it was vitiated by this developmental bias. Books on 'the evolution of Hebrew religion'—to take only one example—are no longer being published, and it is probable that even such a volume as Oesterley and Robinson's, mentioned above, should now be read with a certain wariness.

This means that historians have recovered their sense of the discontinuous element in history, the element which cannot be explained in terms of the unfolding of human nature, but must be assigned to extraneous or transcendent agencies. An example of how the elements of continuity and discontinuity may have their place side by side in the modern Christian philosophy of history is provided by Professor C. H. Dodd, who writes:

'The story of Israel in the Old Testament can readily be interpreted, and up to a point truly interpreted, as an "evolution of religion". But if it is so considered, the product of that evolution is not Christ, or Christianity, but the Judaism which destroyed Jesus, to its own cost. As Paul acutely pointed out, the history of Israel has a paradoxical character, in that it proceeds from a divine purpose, yet that purpose is apparently frustrated, as the field within which it works, that of the people of God, is progressively narrowed, until at last it is represented by one single individual, who is destroyed by the very institutions through which Israel had kept and developed its identity. In Christ the people of God dies, is crucified to the world. But in Christ the people of God rises from the dead and enters upon newness of life. Not development in time, but death and resurrection, judgement and a new creation, is the character of history—the *Endgeschichte*—in which the purpose of God is brought to fulfilment. The series of events which makes up the history of Israel served to bring about a situation ("the fulness of time") in which the Kingdom of God came upon men. It came as judgement and as redemption, as gift and as challenge. It came as the "wholly other" which yet gives meaning to this world. In other words, history was at that point re-created from an inner centre in which "the powers of the age to come", or of the eternal world, were in action. It was determined, not by the horizontal forces of development within time, but by the vertical impact of forces from the unseen.'[1]

Such a statement allows important place to the idea of development without regarding it as the master-key to all historical meaning. Yet it is only as master-key that it can serve the purposes of a general belief in progress. It might therefore be said that only those who are prepared to accept something like the full Hegelian metaphysic can find in the idea of development, taken by itself, an *a priori* principle capable of this service; for it is Hegel alone who worked out the full implications of the line of thought initiated by Lessing and Herder. And such are nowadays a very small band. Yet even the Hegelian metaphysic is here of somewhat doubtful utility, because, as we have seen, its author has left us uncertain of his meaning on the altogether crucial point of the relation of the logical development of concepts to the chronological order of events. Hegel's own relation to the idea of progress is thus an equivocal one; and it is probably true that his idea of development was found to serve the purpose of a more

[1] In *The Kingdom of God and History*, pp. 33 f. Cf. also Professor Dodd's *History and the Gospel* (1938), pp. 139–42.

confident belief in progress only after it had entered into combination with the later doctrine of evolution. What was really effective was the union of the immanental conception of historical process with the new scientific teaching which substituted continuous process for the creation of static entities in the organic realm.

Something of an exception is the philosophy of Croce. For him also history is a story of immanental development—of the gradual unfolding of ideal values latent in its earlier stages. But he steadfastly refuses to link up this unfolding with the natural process of the emergence of new organic species, and pours scorn on those 'cosmological romances' which 'run on without meeting any obstacle, from the cell, indeed from the nebula, to the French Revolution, and even to the socialist movements of the nineteenth century'.[1] He rejects the idea of universal history, maintaining that only special histories are possible, histories that solve particular problems, answer particular questions, and reveal the unfolding of particular ideas, 'because thought thinks facts to the extent that it discerns a special aspect of them';[2] though on the other hand such special histories are permeated by the universal, since the particular ideas and problems cannot be really isolated from one another as separate entities. Furthermore he is careful to distinguish the idea of development from that of progress by discrete stages, which he rightly believes to have characterized eighteenth-century rationalism and to be still potent in many minds. 'The true solution', he writes, 'is that of progress understood, not

[1] *Theory and History of Historiography*, p. 129 f.   [2] Ibid., p. 121.

as a passage from evil to good, as though from one state to another, but as the passage from the good to the better, in which the evil is the good itself seen in the light of the better.'[1] Yet he is able to affirm the reality of such progress only by the device of refusing to regard either natural catastrophes or evils due to human agency as a proper subject of history, except in so far as they can be seen to have been subservient to the development of later good. This very elusive position cannot safely be stated save in his own words:

'History is about the positive and not about the negative, about what man does and not what he suffers. The negative is certainly correlated to the other, but just because of this it does not enter the picture otherwise than through this correlation and in virtue of this office, and may never become itself the subject. Man's action combats obstructing beliefs and tendencies, conquers them, overcomes them, reduces them to mere stuff for his handling, and on this man rears himself up. The historian never loses sight of the work achieved among these obstacles and with these efforts and with these means. Even when some work has completed its life cycle and become decadent and dies, he gazes not upon the decadence and death, but upon the new work that is being prepared within this decadence, where it is already sown and will grow in future and bear fruit. . . . Both the natural disasters which fall upon human communities, like earthquakes, volcanic eruptions, floods, and epidemics, and the disasters men inflict upon themselves, like invasions, massacres, thefts and plunderings, and the wickedness, treachery and cruelty that offend the soul of man, all these may fill human memory with grief, horror and indignation, but they do not merit the interest of the historian (who, in these matters, verges upon the epic and the heroic) except as they provide the incentives and the material for generous human activity in which alone he is interested. . . . All this creativeness, and it alone, is the true subject of history.'[2]

[1] Ibid., p. 85.   [2] *History as the Story of Liberty*, p. 161 f.

Now whether such a contention assumes the reality of general human progress, or merely by-passes the question of it, may be extremely difficult to say; but it certainly does nothing to establish it.

§ 30

We thus come down to the layer of onion-skin represented by the rationalism of the seventeenth and eighteenth centuries; the rationalism of the Baconian and especially the Cartesian movements; the rationalism of the French *philosophes* and Encyclopaedists; not to say that of the Jacobins who in 1792 enthroned a painted Parisienne as the Goddess of Reason in the Cathedral of Notre Dame. We have already seen what was the *a priori* basis of that belief in progress which animated such men as Saint-Pierre, Turgot and Condorcet; it was a confidence in the omnicompetence of human reason to solve all our human problems. There was as yet no idea, such as the German thinkers were afterwards to introduce, of the predetermined development of the human spirit, but rather a reliance upon the free application of expanding human knowledge. It was believed, not without good foundation, that the history of the race was marked by a steady increase of factual and technical knowledge; but it was further assumed that such increase must be accompanied *pari passu* with increase in welfare. The problem of human perfectibility, whether individual or social, was thus reduced to an intellectual one. The root of evil is in ignorance, and the secret of salvation is knowledge. A more enlightened education is all that is needed to make men progressively better; and more enlightened government to make society progressively better. The omnicompetence of legislative action is an essential corollary of eighteenth-century belief in the omnicompetence of rational persuasion.

Here indeed is an *a priori* principle sufficient to justify belief in progress. But is it really available to us? We cannot think so. What the eighteenth century failed to realize has now been powerfully brought home to us by twentieth-century experience, namely, that every advance in knowledge is as capable of being used for evil as for good, and that our choice between the two uses is determined by elements in human nature other than the merely cognitive. Of course if knowledge were here understood in the profound sense of, for instance, the Pauline and Johannine *gnosis*, or even of the Socratic 'Know thyself', this statement might require qualification. But it is not of such knowledge that the seventeenth and eighteenth centuries were thinking, when they felt themselves able to claim that it had in fact increased with the passage of time. They were thinking of technical knowledge, of such an understanding of the behaviour of external nature as enabled man to turn it to his own uses; and the proof of this is that their favourite examples were the invention of gunpowder, the mariner's compass and the printing-press.[1]

[1] Bury quotes a passage from Bacon instancing these three examples, and adds: 'We have seen that these three examples had already been classed together as outstanding by Cardan and Le Roy. They also appear in Companella. Bodin, as we saw, includes them in a longer list.'—*The Idea of Progress*, p. 54 n.

Had they lived in our own time, their most up-to-date examples would doubtless have been the aeroplane and the release of atomic energy.

What is true is that every such triumph of human discovery increases man's power over his own destiny. Nevertheless in themselves these are all ethically ambivalent, as capable of being used for evil as for good, for unhappiness as for felicity, for destruction as for salvation; and we are still left in the dark as to any *a priori* ground of confidence that they are more likely to be used for the latter ends than for the former. And has recent history, the history that has followed on the heels of that Age of Reason, given us any *a priori* ground of confidence? Few will be bold enough to affirm it. The printing-press? Has it not lately been shown to be at least as mighty a force in the service of the powers of darkness as of the powers of light? Gunpowder? Will any say that its influence has been more upbuilding than destroying? The mariner's compass? Has that been used to guide us to the right rather than to the wrong havens? The aeroplane? Dr. Reinhold Niebuhr quotes a scientist as having recently remarked that 'The superman built the aeroplane, but the ape-man got hold of it'.[1] And as for atomic energy, we cannot but have it in our minds that at least its first use was to make a bomb which killed many thousands of men, women and children, and that we are still living in fear and trembling lest the continuance of its destructive use should outpace the development of its beneficent potencies.

[1] *Human Nature* (1941), p. 281.

The general error of rationalism lay in its exclusive stress upon the discursive intellect to the neglect of the other powers of the human spirit operative in its adjustment to reality. The particular error of the rationalist belief in progress lay in its assumption that the advance of discursive intellectual knowledge would be enough to ensure the advance of the whole spirit of man. This mistake was made because the signal intellectual triumphs of the period, the triumphs which most clearly marked an advance on the knowledge of earlier ages, were in the realm of the physical sciences, and because too facile an analogy was drawn between the physical and moral spheres. But in adjusting ourselves to our physical environment only part of our personality is brought into play. Only to a minor degree are the investigations of the natural scientist, or the skills of the technician, interfered with by his personal hopes and fears, loves and hates, ambitions and jealousies. On the other hand, in our relations with our human environment these further elements of our total personality are given the fullest opportunity to influence the result. Whereas, therefore, the merely technical progress of civilization may to a large extent be assured by the advance of knowledge, something quite different is required to ensure moral and social progress. The hindrance now is not that we do not know enough, but that we are not good enough to use what knowledge we have in the service of the best ends. The error of the rationalists was to envisage the progress of society as a problem of the intellect, whereas we now see it to be fundamentally a problem of the will and of the affections.

Technical advance does indeed make a difference to the social scene, but it does this rather by changing the terms of the social problem than by ensuring its solution. With the advance of technical invention—in the change from hunting to pastoral and then to agricultural methods of food-getting, in the discovery of more rapid means of travel, and so on—the social units standing in need of harmonious cohesion have increased in size, from the phratry to the tribe, from the tribe to the nation, from the nation to the United Nations. But, as we are at the moment so acutely conscious, something entirely different from technical invention is required to ensure that the larger unit *will* harmoniously cohere.

We are thus forced to the conclusion that the *a priori* presupposition, the element of faith, which was the specific foundation of seventeenth-century and eighteenth-century belief in progress, is no longer available to us. And it is principally because this lamp is shattered and its light in the dust lies dead, that that belief itself is now beginning to disappear from the minds of our contemporaries. It is not nearly so much the doubts recently cast on the legitimacy of the wider applications of the doctrine of evolution, nor yet the diminished prestige of the Hegelian idea of development, that have brought about this result, as the failure of the belief that men are likely to turn their advancing knowledge to greater personal and social good. It is, of course, among our keen-minded intellectuals that the change of outlook is chiefly to be remarked. The generality of men still cherish the comforting belief, but, since these can usually be counted upon to follow where the more thoughtful spirits lead, it is unlikely that they will continue to cherish it for very long, unless some new and unexpected movement of thought should be found to interfere.

And this is a prospect in which none can be so insensitive or hard-hearted as to rejoice; a situation the possible disastrous consequences of which it is difficult to overestimate. For what, after all, is left for modern man to believe in, if he can no longer believe that the future is likely to be better than the past, or that his children's children are likely to inhabit a world less full of wrong than he himself has had to live in? We have all of us, we children of the modern West, nourished this illusion in our breasts, if illusion indeed it be; and we are all involved together in the tragedy of its fading. Or if indeed there be a few who have never nourished it, even they will hardly have the heart to cry 'I told you so'.

But perhaps it is not all illusion. There is still the core of the onion to be considered, and we have seen that this core, however diminished, consists in certain ideas derived from original Christianity. We saw also that in being thus taken up into the faith of modern progressivism each of these ideas suffered a certain modification. Perhaps this core may still be available to us, and perhaps it may leave to us an optimism sufficient for our most urgent need. Or perhaps, if it is indeed available, yet not in its traditional form entirely sufficient, we may discover that some thin layer of modern progressivist thought still clings to it in such modification or extension of the traditional teaching as finds a degree of justification in the original Gospel message. That would mean that modern progressivism has helped Christian thought to the attainment of an insight which, however absent from its patristic and medieval formulations, is none the less proper to its own original substance, and that so much at least of the belief in progress can appeal to the whole Christian system as its ultimate *a priori* foundation.

§ 31

Meanwhile, and in preparation for our discussion of this final problem, we must raise a further question regarding modern progressivism. We must ask whether in its familiar form, as determined by its rejection of many leading Christian ideas and its consequent distortion of those others by which it has allowed itself to be influenced, it could ever, even if substantiated, provide the spiritual satisfaction which men have sought in it. There are weighty reasons for believing that it could not.

Some of these reasons apply more to its gradualist than to its revolutionary forms. It is characteristic of such gradualism to ignore the Christian ideas of consummation and fulfilment, yet the truth is that these are strictly necessary to the completion of its own thought. It therefore seems unlikely that men will much longer continue to take pleasure in a conception of progress that is detached from all conception of culmination, that is, in a forward movement that leads to no goal. The nineteenth century did indeed take pleasure in it, enjoying the reaction from the traditional Christian teaching which dreamed only of the heavenly goal and made little or nothing of the possibilities of earthly betterment. The new mood, deriving from the *Aufklärung*, is already typified by Lessing's celebrated remark that, if God offered him a choice between the possession of truth and the quest of it, he would unhesitatingly prefer the latter; as well as by Kant's changed conception of immortal life as endless advance towards a perfection that can never actually be attained. The later expressions of it in English nineteenth-century literature are almost too trite to require citation—Carlyle's glorification of labour for its own sake, Tennyson's lines about the great world spinning for ever down the ringing grooves of change, Stevenson's declaration that 'To be truly happy is a question of how we begin and not of how we end, of what we want and not of what we have; . . . for to travel hopefully is a better thing than to arrive, and the true success is to labour.'[1] Such protestations have not worn well, and already seem very threadbare. All earlier thought had associated endlessness with a settled state of being, and the state of becoming with a limited period of time; but what we are here asked to contemplate is an endless becoming such as never attains to being. What is retained from the Christian tradition is the thought of history as having direction; what is cast aside is the thought of it as reaching destination. But in this way the significance Christianity gave to history is lost. History can retain significance only so long as it is conceived to lead to some definite and attainable goal.

The revolutionary versions of progressivism show a

[1] *Virginibus Puerisque*, 'El Dorado'.

realistic awareness of this fact, and are in this respect superior to the gradualist, refusing their will-o'-the-wisp consolations. But in another respect they are less realist, because they allow themselves to cherish the belief that the perfect state of being is attainable within the confines of earthly history. What is here retained from the Christian tradition is the thought of history as leading to a consummation; what is cast aside is the clear realization that this consummation itself must itself be beyond history. But the element of illusion contained in such views is so manifest as to make their long-continued entertainment very unlikely. Even if the pattern of social life of which the revolutionary dreams could be swiftly attained, and then indefinitely maintained, he must soon awake to the realization that our deepest human needs are still unmet, our profoundest desires unsatisfied, our most tragic ills unvanquished. *Omnis qui bibit ex aqua hac sitiet iterum.*

There is, however, a further serious weakness in the conception of progress, which is equally manifest in both versions of it, namely, its willingness to sacrifice the earlier to the later generations of men on the earth. It invites us to find our ultimate spiritual satisfaction in the contemplation of a future breed who will enjoy the things for which we can only yearn and strive. It elevates some future generation to the status of an end in itself, and degrades all earlier generations to the status of mere means to that end. But such a proposal runs too manifestly counter to our deepest moral divinings to yield the satisfaction it promises. Because we are impelled by these divinings to regard the individual personality as the real bearer of value, we cannot be lured into cheerfulness by a solution of our human problem which thus promises fulfilment to some and denies it to others. The only alternative to pessimism lies in the ability to believe that the prospect of fulfilment is open to every human soul of every human generation, that to none is denied the possibility of the life which is life indeed. Those varieties of optimism which have attempted to maintain themselves by ignoring the generations that perish by the way, must ultimately reveal their bankruptcy; leading perhaps to the retraversing by modern thought of the path long ago followed by the Hebrew mind when, in the last centuries before Christ, it was awakened to the hope of a heavenly consummation in which not merely some generation yet unborn, but all the generations of the forefathers, should fully participate.

The most deep-seated weakness of modern progressivism is thus not in the difficulty of establishing the fact of such progress as it affirms, but in our inability to derive from the contemplation of that fact, even if established, the comfort it proposes to administer. We can take final comfort neither from a history that is never consummated nor from any consummation that earthly history itself could conceivably contain. An earthly state of being in which there is nothing left to strive for is as unmeaning to us as one in which we are bidden to strive for mere striving's sake. Nor again can we be content to limit the enjoyment of the consummation to some fortunate future race, finding in the life of some distant to-morrow the justification of the life of both yesterday and to-day, and allowing to each present moment no direct relation of its own to eternity but only a relation that passes through future time.[1]

[1] With this section compare N. Berdyaev, *The Meaning of History* (English translation, 1936), pp. 187 ff.

CHAPTER V

TOWARDS A CONCLUSION

§ 32

'THAT we think of progress at all', writes Professor John Macmurray in *The Clue to History*, 'shows the extent of the influence of Christianity upon us. That we think of it as a natural process of evolution shows how far we still are from any adequate comprehension of Christianity.' Historical progress, this author explains, differs from natural evolution in being an intentional activity towards a foreseen end, and also in involving the intentional co-operation of different individuals towards the same end. Human history can therefore be thought of as progressive only if it is in some sort conceived as a single action. But the conception of history as a single action involves the conception of a universal agent, that is, of God. Moreover, the achievement of progress depends on the identification of the wills of men with the will of God towards the determined end, the divine intention becoming so far also a human intention. 'Thus it is clear that the idea of progress can have no other origin than the Jewish one, and that it is an essentially Christian conception which can have no rational basis save in a religious consciousness of the world.'[1]

Such is the thesis of Professor Macmurray's book and, without necessarily committing ourselves to all that he

[1] Op. cit., pp. 113–15.

186

says in elaboration of it, we may welcome its clear formulation of a conclusion to which our own argument has
led us.[1] There is now no room for doubt that the spring
of modern belief in progress is to be looked for in the
Biblical conception of history as moving forwards towards a goal worthy of heart's desire. There is almost as
little doubt that the various alternative *a priori* presuppositions with which in the modern mind this conception
has been supplied in replacement of the original Christian
presupposition of the providential guidance of history
towards the salvation of the race—namely, the inevitable
issuance of intellectual enlightenment in moral betterment, the Hegelian principle of development, and the

---

[1] We may cite also T. H. Green's defence, in his *Prolegomena to Ethics*
(1883), § 189, of the thesis that 'If there is a progress in the history of
men, it must be towards an end consisting in a state of being which is not
itself a series in time, but is both comprehended eternally in the eternal
mind and is intrinsically, or in itself eternal.' Or again R. G. Collingwood's
argument in *The Idea of History* (1946), p. 48 f., that Christianity introduced
a new attitude to history 'according to which the historical process is the
working out not of man's purposes but of God's. . . . Thus each human
agent knows what he wants and pursues it, but he does not know why he
wants it: the reason why he wants it is that God has caused him to want it
in order to advance the process of realizing His purpose. In one sense man
is the agent throughout history, for everything that happens in history happens by his will; in another sense God is the sole agent, for it is only by the
working of God's providence that the operation of man's will at any given
time leads to *this* result, and not to a different one. . . . By this new attitude
to human action history gained enormously. . . . This new view of history
makes it possible to see not only the actions of historical agents, but the
existence and nature of these agents themselves, as vehicles of God's purpose
and therefore historically important. . . . This was a profound revolution in
historical thinking; it meant that the process of historical change was no
longer conceived as flowing, so to speak, over the surface of things, and
affecting their accidents only, but as involving their real substance and thus
entailing a real creation and a real destruction.'

extension of the principle of organic evolution to the field of free human action—now find themselves helpless to resist the acids of contemporary scepticism. It therefore becomes urgent to enquire whether the original Christian presupposition itself, if accepted, provides ground for the retention of some kind of optimistic outlook on future earthly history.

The pattern provided for history in the Bible is at the same time a universal and a particular one. It covers the destiny of all men and nations, yet finds the key to the forward movement of the whole in the destiny of a single community and in a single sequence of events. The Biblical writers all believe that the only really significant thing about the life of any man or nation is the relation in which it stands to the promises of God which were made in the first place to the national community of Israel; the later prophets teaching that the 'faithful remnant' rather than the whole people is the true successor of this original community and the consequent heir of the promises; while the apostolic writers teach that the fellowship of Christ's followers is continuous with that faithful remnant, and that in its life the promises are now being fulfilled. It is a slender strand of events that is here being traced for us down the ages, but the outlook is on cosmic history as a whole, this narrow strand being held to enclose God's purpose for all men everywhere and indeed for the whole of His creation. 'In those days', says the prophet, looking forward, 'it shall come to pass that ten men from nations of every language shall take hold of the skirt of one Jew, saying, We will go with you, for we have heard that God is with you.'[1] 'That was the true Light', says the evangelist, looking backwards, 'that enlightens every man', and 'to as many as received Him He gave power to become the sons of God'.[2]

The original Christian hope, which provided the starting-point for modern progressivism, is thus a hope radiating from a single centre and existing only for those whose lives are determined by a positive relation to that centre. Hence the only progress that could have meaning for original Christianity is the progressive embodiment in humanity of the Spirit of Christ.

Yet, as we saw in an earlier chapter, the hope of which the New Testament primarily speaks seems to be conceived in quite other terms than these. What we find there is a conjunction of the sense of present fulfilment with the expectation of that final glory in which history will one day culminate. On the one hand there is the conviction that *finita iam sunt proelia*, and that on the basis of Christ's victory and the Pentecostal descent of the Spirit a new kind of life is opened up to mankind—a life which is already beginning to be lived within the narrow limits of the Christian community. On the other hand, this consciousness of present fruition is everywhere balanced by an acute sense of the limitations and disabilities which still remain, yet these ills are realized to be of a kind that cannot possibly be relieved by any further movement of earthly history, but only when that history, reaching its term, shall have yielded place to the perfect

[1] Zech. viii. 23.　　　　[2] John i. 9–12.

189

blessedness of the heavenly Kingdom. When the New Testament speaks of hope, it is therefore this ultimate hope that is primarily in mind. 'For our citizenship (or commonwealth, πολίτευμα) is in heaven, and from heaven we await a Saviour, the Lord Jesus Christ, who will transform the body of our humiliation, to be like the body of His glory, by the power which enables Him to subject all things to Himself.'[1] The words are as emphatic and unambiguous as they are typical of the whole apostolic temper. Nor have we any alternative but to consent to the admirable realism which thus rejoices with joy unspeakable over the amplitude of the new life that is already possible in Christ, without for a moment closing its eyes to the tragically restricting limitations within which that life must now be lived, and without ever harbouring the illusion that these can be removed while terrestrial conditions remain. But the question which now emerges, having been forcibly suggested to us by the appearance of modern progressivism, is whether there is in original Christianity also another kind of hope, namely, the hope that during the interim period, the years of grace falling between the inauguration of the Christian era and the end of earthly history, human life and society will be more and more conformed to the mind of Christ.

We have already noticed how slenderly any expectation of this kind is represented in the Christian thought of the later patristic and medieval periods—how largely the life of the present 'dispensation' was then conceived

[1] Phil. iii. 20 f.

in static terms.[1] but there is a reason why we should hesitate to regard this negative judgement as in any way final. It is not only that these ages had little or nothing of any kind to say in answer to this more restricted question, but that they altered the balance of the New Testament teaching in a way which virtually prevented them from raising it. In the first place, the rigidity of their distinction between the present life of the Christian and the promised state of heavenly beatitude was such as to give far less than due notice to what the New Testament has to say about the powers of the new age already inaugurated and the already realized blessedness of life in Christ; so that attention came to be concentrated in far too exclusive a way on the attainment of the future state. Not only, however, was medieval eschatology too futurist; it was also too individualist. The work of Christ tended to be limited to the provision of a means whereby individual souls

---

[1] Some mention may here be expected of Joachim of Flora, the twelfth-century Calabrian monk who divided history into three overlapping dispensations, the Age of the Father extending from Adam to Christ, the Age of the Son extending from Uzziah to the year A.D. 1260, and the Age of the Spirit extending from St. Benedict to the end of the world. The significant part of this scheme lies in Joachim's belief that in his own time a new chapter in the history of revelation and in the life of man, which had been inaugurated by the founding of the monastic orders, was about to reach the stage of fructification and would then continue for ever. Here undoubtedly we have a conception, not only of progressive revelation, but of a certain forward move *within* the Christian period. But it is a *single* forward move, and it is not only fantastically but also narrowly conceived, as a sort of change-over from an age of clerics to an age of monks. The doctrine was condemned by the Synod of Arles in 1263, but continued to have influence among the Spirituals of the Franciscan Order. See Henry Bett, *Joachim of Flora* (1931); C. G. Coulton, *From St. Francis to Dante* (2nd edition, 1907), chapter xiii.

secure entrance to paradise after the death of the body, and neither the cosmic nor the community aspect of the Christian salvation was allowed the place accorded to it in the New Testament. It is, however, precisely these aspects of New Testament thought that recent scholarship has been most concerned to investigate, and it is not until we have reckoned with the results of such researches that the way is cleared for our particular question.

§ 33

The conception of the Kingdom of God had played a prominent part in the theological thought of the nine-teenth century, but the use made of it was much coloured by the activist and progressivist temper of the age. Al-brecht Ritschl, the most influential Protestant theologian of the second half of the century, in elevating this concep-tion to a central place in his system, understood it to mean the kind of life in community for the establishment of which God works in the world and desires the co-opera-tion of men. It is 'the *summum bonum* which God realizes in men; and at the same time it is their common task, since it is only through the rendering of obedience on man's part that God's sovereignty possesses continuous existence.'[1] As this employment of the term gained cur-rency, its relation to the use made of it in the teaching of Jesus was eagerly investigated by New Testament scholars. It was generally concluded that Jesus sometimes spoke of the Kingdom as an order of things to be intro-

[1] *Justification and Reconciliation*, Vol. III, English translation, p. 30.

duced by God at the end of earthly history, but sometimes also as an immanent reality already present in the
hearts of believers and through their agency gradually
permeating the society of men; but it was confidently
felt that the former represented the Judaistic cabinet in
which Jesus' teaching was set, and the latter His own real
view. As Adolf Harnack declared in 1899 to a large audi-
ence of students in the University of Berlin:

'Jesus' message of the Kingdom of God runs through all the forms
and statements of the prophecy which, taking its colour from the
Old Testament, announces the day of judgement and the visible
government of God in the future, up to the idea of an inward coming
of the Kingdom, starting with Jesus' message and then beginning.
His message embraces these two poles, with many stages between
them that shade off one into another. At the one pole the coming
of the Kingdom seems to be a purely future event; at the other,
it appears as something inward, something already present and
making its entrance at the moment. . . . There can be no doubt
that [the former] was an idea which Jesus simply shared with His
contemporaries. He did not start it, but He grew up in it and He
retained it. The other view, that the Kingdom of God "cometh
not with observation", that it is already here, was His own.[1]

Already in 1892, however, Johannes Weiss had published a pamphlet of sixty-seven pages[2] in which, as the
result of careful exegesis of the material in the Synoptic
Gospels, he concluded that Jesus conceived of the Kingdom in no other way than as a wholly future and supernal
order of things to be inaugurated by God's power at the
end of earthly history and after a Day of Judgement

[1] *What is Christianity?* (English translation of *Das Wesen des Christentums*),
pp. 53–5.
[2] *Die Predigt Jesu vom Reiche Gottes.*

which, though He disclaimed any knowledge of its exact timing, He nevertheless mistakenly believed would fall within the lifetime of the generation then living. In 1906 Dr. Albert Schweitzer, in his *Quest of the Historical Jesus*,[1] brought his own genius and a further weight of learning to the support of an identical conclusion.

The excitement caused by this apparent historical discovery was very great. Yet it is noteworthy that for Weiss himself it remained merely, and for Dr. Schweitzer little more than, an historical discovery. Neither was able to accept for himself the outlook which scholarly integrity obliged them to attribute to Jesus. The thinking of Weiss continued to be entirely, and that of Dr. Schweitzer almost entirely, dominated by the outlook of nineteenth-century liberalism. In 1901 the former wrote in the preface to his second edition that though the Ritschlian conception of the Kingdom is very different from that of Jesus, yet he himself was still of opinion that Ritschl's usage of the term is best suited to make the Christian religion intelligible to men and to awaken and foster a healthy religious life.[2] While the latter concluded his book by saying that, when the adjustment necessitated by the new conclusions is faithfully made, 'the historical Jesus will be to our time a stranger and an enigma'. He added only that this very strangeness is in some ways a blessing in disguise, since 'it is not Jesus as historically known, but Jesus as spiritually arisen within men, who is significant

---

[1] Entitled in the first German edition *Von Reimarus zu Wrede*. The argument of this book was, however, anticipated in the same writer's *Messianitäst-und Leidensgeheimnis*, published in 1901.

[2] Op. cit., p. v.

for our time and can help it. . . . The abiding and eternal in Jesus is absolutely independent of historical knowledge, and can only be understood by contact with His spirit which is still at work in the world.'[1]

An example of a different reaction is, however, to be found in Father George Tyrrell's *Christianity at the Cross-Roads*, which appeared posthumously in 1909 under the direct inspiration of Dr. Schweitzer's book. However much a 'Modernist' in other ways, Tyrrell broke completely with the activist and progressivist strains in modern liberalism. Unlike Weiss and Dr. Schweitzer, his outlook on the future terrestrial history of the race was radically pessimist.

'The verdict of the deeper spiritual intuition on this life is always pessimistic, and it is a verdict that is only confirmed by experience and reflection. It is evident that there are vital and progressive forces at work everywhere, but it is equally plain that there are destructive forces, that life is strangled by its own fertility, that it is faced by the insoluble problem of finding room for its own expansion, that the utmost its ingenuity can do is to defer the inevitable day of defeat and to prolong its periods of uninterrupted progress. The world is the arena of a conflict between a multitude of irreconcilable ends. The belief that they are ordained to an eventual harmony, however useful as a stimulus to combat, falls to pieces on closer inspection, which reveals an inherent rift in nature. All life is under the sway of sad mortality.'[2]

Tyrrell therefore welcomes the new apocalyptic reading of the hope of Jesus as offering us a much more realistic picture of our human situation than the progressivist reading was able to do. Only it must be understood not

[1] Op. cit., English translation, p. 399.
[2] Op. cit., p. 119 f.

literally but symbolically, as typifying the reality of a transcendent world which lies alongside the world of time and space, and in which alone our hopes must find their anchorage.

A useful link with the next stage of the discussion is provided by the consideration of Tyrrell's book contained in an essay on 'Human Progress' by the late Edwyn Bevan, which appeared in 1921. After summarizing Tyrrell's position Bevan continues:

'This view is not one which commends itself to me, but I think it is worthy of serious consideration. I think the current optimism is largely so unreflective and easy-going that it was well it should be challenged. Tyrrell's position is one which, so far as I can see, perfectly preserves the essential part of the Christian or the theistic hope. I feel that if it were proved to me that all attempt to make the world better must fail, I might still be a Christian and ought to strive. But the proof of that view would, I confess, have to be very strong in order to overcome a repugnance I feel towards it. I wonder how many people there are whose enthusiasm for a good cause would be in no degree dashed by the discovery that all effort and all self-sacrifice on its behalf would never achieve more than an evanescent result in the world about them.'[1]

'I do not feel that the Christian faith *necessitates* a belief in the progress of humanity upon this planet, in the improvement of the world. . . . Yet it is impossible not to be interested in the question. . . . If we believe in a Divine Purpose, then we must hold that the progress of humanity hitherto . . . has been part of God's design. And if God's design has up till now meant a gradual ascent of man on this planet, that is surely, so far as it goes, a reason for anticipating that God's design will involve an analogous ascent from stage to stage in the future. This globe may be only the platform which mankind crosses, and the true history of mankind may follow the

[1] *Hellenism and Christianity* (1921), p. 198 f.

line of his passage into the Unseen, not the succession of generations upon earth. Granted, and yet the earth too, as the sacred vehicle of man's spirit in this phase of its being, may have a history of its own, guided to a worthy end.'[1]

In another essay, written nearly twenty years later, Bevan recurred to the same theme, and again used the metaphor of the platform; but he now seemed distinctly less hospitable towards the hope of earthly progress. He does not forbid us to entertain such a hope. 'There is no reason to suppose that attempts to bring about a juster, a happier, a wiser world are necessarily condemned beforehand to futility.' Yet we can have 'no assurance . . . that earthly conditions will actually become better before the end of history'; and it is only 'the heavenly hope which is essential to Christianity'.[2] In the true Christian outlook,

'the passage of humanity appears not as a passage along the line of earthly history, to an ultimate goal on earth, but as a passage *across* the line of earthly history, the earth being only a platform which each generation crosses obliquely from birth to its entrance, individual by individual, into the unseen world, the world always there beside the visible one. The formation of the Divine Community in that unseen world is the supreme hope, in comparison with which everything which happens on this temporal platform, now or in the future, is of minor importance.

'Whenever the main stress is laid upon "building Jerusalem in England's green and pleasant land", the Christian attitude to the world is abandoned.'[3]

The question now is whether such a statement takes up

[1] Ibid., pp. 197, 199 f.
[2] *The Kingdom of God and History* (1938, Oxford Conference Series), p. 56 f.
[3] Ibid., p. 56 f.

into itself the whole message of the New Testament. Or perhaps we should rather say, of the Bible as a whole. For the writings of the Old Testament prophets have always been held to be, in their own way and place, as truly a part of our original Christian heritage as, say, the Book of Revelation; and it may very reasonably be contended that the prophetic temper, no less than the apocalyptic, has its own distinctive contribution to make to the Christian thought of these years of grace. It is probable that the transition from prophecy to apocalypse within the Judaistic period, while mainly determined by a true deepening of insight into the relations of the temporal and the eternal, was also partly conditioned by the change that had now overtaken the fortunes of Israel, issuing in what may be regarded as the final[1] defeat of her nationalist aspirations at the hands of Alexander on the battlefield of Issus in 333 B.C. It is usually held that the transition from the Platonic and Aristotelian to the Stoic (and, more generally, the Hellenistic) outlook, which Dr. Gilbert Murray has characterized as 'a failure of nerve',[2] was partly determined by the defeat of Greek nationalist aspirations, only five years earlier, at the hands of Alexander's father on the battlefield of Chaeronaea; and it may be that there is some degree—we should not suggest more—of parallelism between the two cases. Of the powerful influence of this apocalyptic outlook on the minds of the first Christians there can be no doubt, and there can be as

[1] Or perhaps the word 'final' should be reserved for Pompey's capture of Jerusalem in 65 B.C.

[2] *Five Stages of Greek Religion*, Preface and Chapter IV. Dr. Murray explains that he originally had the phrase from Bury.

little doubt that from it Christianity gained much that became part of its very being. Yet it was natural that when the promise 'Lo, I come quickly' was thought to mean that the end of all things would come within the lifetime of the existing generation, this apocalyptic element should often take precedence over everything else. And perhaps it is equally natural that, in an age when Christians know the period of earthly history to have been at least so far extended as to cover another two millennia, these should find in the prophetic outlook some encouragement for their hopes of the terrestrial future such as they could hardly derive from the apocalyptic. But there is still more to be said. The deepest reason why the early Christians had less to say about the future of earthly society than had the prophets of Israel was not their mistaken foreshortening of its period, but the fact that they had no present voice or vote in the general affairs of that society. St. Paul addressed his epistles to little groups of men and women who were endeavouring to live the true Christian life in the midst of a vast and powerful, but wholly alien and pagan, society and suited what he had to say to their current needs and problems. It is therefore unfair to expect from these epistles a direct answer to the further questions which inevitably suggest themselves to the mind, because they arise out of the circumstances, of those who like ourselves possess both voice and vote and have accordingly as much responsibility as anybody else for the human direction of affairs of the *respublica terrena*.

But though we must not demand a direct answer, we

have a right to expect from the New Testament some indication of the principles on which our own answer must be based. Hence the more important question is whether even the whole of the specifically New Testament teaching is taken up into such a statement as Bevan's. It is here that the latest developments of New Testament scholarship come especially to our help. No doubt it is true that the New Testament regards the earthly scene as a platform *across* which men pass obliquely one by one into an unseen world which is 'always there' alongside, so that, as a modern poet has it, 'soul by soul and silently her shining bounds increase'.[1] Yet it may be suspected that the elevation of this picture into a position of primacy is more characteristic of a certain strain in later thought than of the New Testament itself. Surely the dominating picture throughout the New Testament is rather of the earth as a platform *along* which men walk, and on which one generation succeeds another, enjoying even now the blessings of a life hid with Christ in God, and waiting in hope for a fullness of glory which will supervene upon the close, not of each individual biography, but of earthly history itself, when the platform will finally be swept away to make room for a new heavens and a new earth. Ample consideration is indeed given to the destiny of those saints who meanwhile die. 'But I would not have you to be ignorant, brethren, concerning them which are asleep,'[2] wrote St. Paul in the very earliest of his extant epistles. But what he then proceeds to say is set within

[1] Sir Cecil Spring-Rice, 'I vow to thee, my country'.
[2] I Thess. iv. 13.

the frame of the larger question of the corporate destiny of the holy community as a whole and of the historical platform itself.[1]

There are indeed two vitally constituent elements of the New Testament outlook that seem to be given less than their due weight in Bevan's statement; elements to which, it is true, equally scant justice was done in the tradition of the later Patristic, the Middle, and the Reformation ages; but to which we have recently been recalled. One is the cosmic aspect of the Christian hope; the other is the sense of a victory already accomplished, and of powers of the Spirit already available to us.

The cosmic significance of the salvation wrought in Christ continued to dominate the Christian mind in the early period, when Greek was still the language of theology. Bishop Aulén has reminded us[2] that, however crude may seem the theory of the atonement then current, whereby the death of Christ was conceived as a price paid by God to the devil in order to buy back mankind out of the devil's power, such a view at least retained the New Testament conviction that the power of evil had already been broken and the consequent keen looking forward, along the path of history, towards its triumphant end. Moreover, these notes continued to be more characteristic of the Greek or Eastern Church than of the Latin or

[1] Cf. O. Cullmann, *Christus und die Zeit*, p. 205: 'Die Zukunft des einzelnen Menschen hängt nach der urchristlichen Erwartung ganz und gar von der Zukunft der gesamten Heilsgeschichte ab . . . In Wirklichkeit steht durchaus nicht das ego in Vordergrund dieser Hoffnung, sondern die Vollendung der ganzen Heilsgeschichte.'

[2] *Christus Victor* (English translation, 1931).

Western. While the latter tended increasingly to the development of an individualist eschatology which threatened to limit the work of Christ to the provision of a means whereby individual souls might escape the pains of hell and secure entrance into heaven after the death of the body, the former retained a more cosmic eschatology and also a more cosmic conception of Christ's atoning work.[1] In Professor Oliver Quick's remarkable little posthumous volume, *The Gospel of the New World*, we have an attempt to restore something of this lost balance. In the theology of the Middle Ages, he writes:

'the destiny of the individual and its determination at the hour of death, not the regeneration (παλιγγενεσία) and restoration (ἀποκατάστασις) of all things at the Second Advent, comes to hold the central place in eschatological thought. . . . The resurrection of Christ Himself is thought of less as the first-fruits of the new world, the transfigured heaven and earth, than as the assurance that the faithful soul, like its Lord, will rise into heavenly glory after death. . . . A mainly individualistic eschatology has replaced the mainly cosmic eschatology of the Bible. The metaphysical importance of time is found less in connection with world history than in the life story of the individual. Time is thought of less as the process of events whereby God is bringing this world to an end in order to

[1] 'Its cosmic interest, its passionate preoccupation with the thought of Resurrection and the Second Coming of Christ, its longing for the glorification of nature as a whole and the salvation of the world by its transfiguration and deification, had already found expression in the Eastern fathers. An Origen, a St. Gregory of Nyssa, were typical of the East. And the doctrine of a salvation exclusively personal, of heaven for the saved and hell for the lost, were equally products of the West. As a result of his psychological constitution the Oriental Christian has placed in the foreground of his religion the question of the Apocatastasis, the restitution of all things; the Western Christian, whether Catholic or Protestant, the question of justification by faith and good works.'—Karl Pfleger, *Wrestlers with Christ* (English translation, 1936), p. 275.

establish the glorious and perfect universe of the world to come; it is thought of more as the process whereby each individual soul reaches its destiny in heaven or hell. . . . The great transformation of the universe at the last day, for which the first Christians had so eagerly looked and waited, seems almost to become an irrelevance; it is hard to fit it in logically to the mediaeval cosmology.'[1]

If we now turn to consider the second of our two missing emphases, we are again helped by Quick. It was not only to the thought of the future, but also of the present, triumph of Christ that he desired to recall us. In Mediaevalism, he wrote,

'the full implications of Christ's resurrection as St. Paul understood them, that through the risen and triumphant Christ *agapē* can permeate and spiritualize every corner of human activity, outward as well as inward, secular as well as religious, and that by this permeation the Church here and now anticipates the life of the world to come, have been obscured. We miss the paean of world-conquest and world-redemption in the whole Body of Christ glorified.'[2]

It is precisely at this point that one of the most notable new movements in contemporary New Testament criticism, the movement indicated by the phrase 'realized eschatology' and associated particularly with the name of Dr. C. H. Dodd, has sought to bring in its contribution. We have here a remarkable turning of the tables against the purely futurist eschatology ascribed to Jesus and His disciples by Weiss and Schweitzer. In the same volume as contains Bevan's later essay Dr. Dodd writes that 'The Kingdom of God is not something yet to come. It came with Jesus Christ.'[3] 'For the New Testament writers in

[1] Op. cit. (1944), pp. 71-3.
[2] Ibid., p. 74.
[3] *The Kingdom of God and History*, p. 35.

general', he says elsewhere, 'the *eschaton* has entered history; the hidden rule of God has been revealed; the Age to Come has come. The Gospel of primitive Christianity is a Gospel of realized eschatology.'[1] 'In the New Testament', he writes in still another volume, 'the Kingdom of God is not (whatever it may be in the Old Testament) identified with the remote goal of history.'[2] There does indeed remain 'a residue of eschatology which is not exhausted in the "realized eschatology" of the Gospel, namely, the element of sheer finality. . . . Thus the idea of a second coming of Christ appears along with the emphatic assertion that His coming in history satisfies all the conditions of the eschatological event, *except* that of absolute finality.'[3] But it would seem that this finality is not to be looked for in a future that will supervene upon the temporal end of history, but rather in a timeless eternal world; and at this point Dr. Dodd's view is very reminiscent of Bevan's, though his emphasis on the present realization of the Kingdom makes his total outlook very different. The New Testament does indeed place the historical process between a Creation at the beginning and a Last Judgement and Second Advent at the end, but ac-

[1] *The Apostolic Preaching and Its Developments* (1936), p. 210. Again in his book, *The Parables of the Kingdom* (1935), he thus summarizes the parabolic teaching of Jesus: 'This is the hour of fulfilment. For many generations the faith of the Jewish people had buoyed itself upon the hope that at long last God would assert His sovereignty in His world, while it sadly confessed that in the present age the powers of evil were strong. In a succession of pictures Jesus declares that the hour has struck and God has acted. The strong man is despoiled; the powers of evil are disarmed. The hidden power of God has manifested itself. . . .' (p. 198).

[2] *History and the Gospel*, p. 181.

[3] *The Apostolic Preaching and Its Developments*, p. 231.

cording to Dr. Dodd this scheme is a mythological one which is not to be understood in any temporal sense. 'The myth of a Last Judgement is a symbolical statement of the final resolution of the great conflict. Serious diffi-culties are raised if we attempt to treat it as a literal and quasi-historical statement that the succession of events in time will one day cease.'[1] Again, 'Doomsday simply takes a cut across the time-stream at any point, and reveals the triumph of the divine purpose in it. But this triumph is something actually attained, not in some coming Day of the Lord, near or distant, but in the concrete historical event of the death and resurrection of Jesus Christ.'[2] At the same time he gives little encouragement to the hope of progress within earthly history. 'The doctrine of pro-gress', he writes, 'which until recently seemed to provide a scheme of interpretation, and of interpretation in a Christian sense, has worn somewhat thin. . . . There are indeed considerations which encourage the hope that the evils of human society are, in the long run, self-destruc-tive, and the good self-preservative. But it is a long way from this to the assurance that history will justify itself by the final victory of the good within the span allotted to human life on this planet. Nor is it clear that the Christian faith intends to give such an assurance.'[3]

What are we to say of this construction? The great gain of it is that it does justice at last to that sense of fulfilment and of victory which dominates the New Testament in

[1] *History and the Gospel*, p. 168.
[2] Ibid., p. 170.
[3] Ibid., p. 180 f.

all its parts. It enables us to understand, for instance, how the writer of the Epistle to the Hebrews could describe Christian believers as 'men who have been once for all enlightened, who have tasted the excellence of the Gospel and the powers of the coming age'.[1] But its great weakness is that it appears to leave hardly any room at all for that other note which the New Testament sounds so clearly, the note of hope. It leaves Christianity with virtually no hope for the future, whether within earthly history or after the end of it—nothing, in fact, beyond such present realization of the dimension of eternity as is already open to us.

What appears a much more faithful account of the relation of hope to fulfilment in the New Testament is offered us in the recent writings of Dr. Oscar Cullmann. He agrees with Dr. Dodd in holding that the primary emphasis is no longer, as in Judaism, upon the future, but upon a fulfilment already granted, a salvation already assured, a victory already won, a new age already inaugurated, and a new quality of life that is therefore now possible. 'It is simply not true to say that early Christianity is eschatologically focused *in the same sense* as Judaism.'[2] On the other hand, the longing for the final consummation not only remains but appears with increased intensity. The Second Advent bulks largely in New Testament thought, but without ever occupying the central position. Indeed 'the criterion of the Christian quality of an apocalypse lies precisely in the question whether it is the cruci-

[1] Heb. vi. 4–5.
[2] *Christus und die Zeit* (1946), p. 73.

fied and risen Christ or the returning Christ that is made to be the centre of the line [of sacred history]'.[1] The earliest Christian confessions, in saying only one thing, did not say that Jesus would one day return to judge the quick and the dead, but that He already reigns as Lord.[2] And Dr. Cullmann comes back again and again to the illustration to which we called attention in an earlier chapter: 'The decisive battle in a war may be fought at a comparatively early stage in the campaign, yet the war may go on for a long time . . . before "Victory Day" comes.'[3] Thus Christianity must always maintain a realized and a futurist eschatology in balance, if never in equipoise. In neglecting the latter it either shuts its eyes to the tragic realities of our continuing warfare or, alternatively, harbours utopian illusions of the possibility of their disappearance from the earthly scene. But in neglecting the former it is failing to understand the specific character, the promise and opportunities, of the years of grace.

§ 34

It will now be understood how necessary it was to acquaint ourselves at such length with these recent developments in the field of New Testament scholarship. For the specific character of the years of grace and the promise attaching to them are precisely the questions we

---

[1] Ibid., p. 78.
[2] *Die ersten christlichen Glaubensbekenntnisse* (1943), pp. 51 ff.
[3] *Christus und die Zeit*, p. 73.

are anxious to investigate, and to which we must now give our close attention.

Here again the writings of Dr. Cullmann are of the greatest help. His careful investigation of the earliest confessional formulae embedded in the New Testament leads him back to the two brief phrases 'Jesus is Lord' and 'Jesus Christ is the Son of God'. These are not, however, independent and separate assertions. Rather does the ascription of Sonship to Jesus serve to explain the fact of His Lordship. What then did the first Christians mean by affirming—and making it the central affirmation of their faith—that Jesus was Lord? They meant that, following His victory over the powers of evil in His death and resurrection, He now rules as King. What they were anxious to do was not to ascribe to Him a merely honorific title, but to declare their conviction that a new age had now come upon the world; and their way of saying this was that, the powers of darkness having been decisively defeated, Jesus had been elevated to the right hand of the Almighty, where He sits as 'the Son of God in power',[1] and whence He now exercises His dominion 'not only over mankind but also over the unseen powers in heaven and on the earth and under the earth'[2]—powers which had hitherto been the rulers of the world.

Dr. Cullmann believes that the New Testament specifically denominates the new age thus introduced as the Kingdom (or Rule, $\beta\alpha\sigma\iota\lambda\epsilon\iota\alpha$) of Christ. This Kingdom is destined to continue until the end of earthly history,

---

[1] Rom. i. 4.
[2] *Die ersten christlichen Glaubensbekenntnisse*, p. 53.

when it will give place to the Kingdom of God which only then will appear in its full power and glory. The period of Christ's Kingdom thus coincides with that of the life of the Christian Church as Christ's earthly embodiment.[1] Certain passages in St. Paul certainly seem to say this:

'For as in Adam all die, so in Christ shall all be made alive. Yet each in his own order: Christ as first fruits, then at Christ's coming all who belong to Him. Then comes the end, when He hands over the Kingdom to God the Father after destroying every ruler and every authority and power. For He must reign until He has put all enemies under His feet. The last enemy to be destroyed is death. . . . When all things are subject to Him, then also the Son himself will be made subject to Him who made all things subject to Him, so that God may be all things to all men.'[2]

'. . . giving thanks to the Father who has enabled us to have a share in the inheritance of the saints in light, and who, rescuing us from the power of darkness, has transferred us to the Kingdom of His beloved Son. . . .'[3]

It is possible that Dr. Cullmann's construction places a little too much weight on these particular passages, but this hardly affects what he has to say generally about the vitally significant place assigned by the New Testament to the *present*, that is, to the years of grace, in the setting of sacred history as a whole—a place that began to be denied to it as early as in the second century, when Irenaeus was already doing his thinking in purely futurist terms.[4]

[1] *Königherrschaft Christi und Kirche im Neuen Testament* (1941).
[2] 1 Cor. xv. 22–8.
[3] Col. i. 12 f.
[4] *Die ersten christlichen Glaubensbekenntnisse*, p. 56.

We are thus fortified in our former conclusion that there is in the New Testament a much greater sense of the transformation of individual and corporate life accomplished by Christ than was taken up in the later Patristic and Medieval tradition. But the question which now remains, and which particularly concerns our present inquiry, is whether this transformation is conceived as likely to be *progressive*. Have the years of grace any interior pattern of their own of a forward-moving kind, or do they form, when regarded qualitatively, a merely static period within the forward movement of the history of salvation? We are agreed that, in addition to enjoying a profound sense of present fulfilment, these years are conceived as animated also by a hope. We are agreed further that this hope has a direction not merely across the platform of earthly history towards a more blessed state of being awaiting those whom death meanwhile calls away from it, but also, and even principally, *along* the platform towards the final consummation of history as a whole after the platform has been swept away. But is there also a hope of better things still to happen on the platform itself?

A positive answer to this question is to be looked for in what the New Testament has to say about the responsibilities, opportunities and prospects of the Christian mission. It is clear that the early Christian outlook on the years of grace is determined entirely by the exigencies of the missionary task. Here lies for it the true significance, the divine rationale, of the interval that must elapse between 'the decisive battle' and 'Victory Day'. It is to this

end that a period of 'grace' has been granted, and it is
for the discharge of this task that it must be used. 'The
good news must first [i.e. before the end] be announced
to all nations.'[1] It cannot be gainsaid that those who thus
set themselves to the missionary task betray every evidence of having supposed that the time available to them
before the end was very short. This, however, makes it
all the more striking to reflect how much they hoped to
accomplish within that time and how widely they essayed
to fling their net. As one New Testament scholar has
written, St. Paul's teaching 'is all based on the conviction
that although the time is short, it will prove sufficient if
only it is employed with an unsparing energy, in the
power of the Spirit'.[2] It may be said that St. Paul's conception of the *orbis terrarum* was a very restricted one and
that if he could have been shown a modern missionary
map, he might have been led to suspect that the end was
not quite so near, and that a longer period of grace would
be granted.[3] But even as it was, the programme he set
himself was sufficiently remarkable.

Now it is quite clear that this conception of the Christian mission not only places the years of grace in a significant relation to the forward movement of sacred history
as a whole, but also provides them with an interior

[1] Mark xiii. 10.
[2] E. F. Scott, *Man and Society in the New Testament* (1946), p. 257.
[3] 'The unification of our present world has long since opened the way for
St. Paul, who once travelled from the Orontes to the Tiber under the aegis
of the *Pax Romana*, to travel on from the Tiber to the Mississippi and from
the Mississippi to the Yangtse'—A. J. Toynbee, *Civilization on Trial* (1948),
p. 239.

directional and progressive pattern of their own. These first Christians were but a small handful of men, among whom were few either noble or learned, in an obscure backwater of the great Roman Empire; yet when they looked forward into such years as lay between them and the end of history, what they saw was the gradual extension of the Rule of Christ among the nations. This was not indeed the only thing they saw; their Lord was believed to have warned them that there would also be wars and rumours of wars, nation rising up against nation and kingdom against kingdom, famines also and earthquakes, many sufferings and persecutions, and the appearance of false Christs who would lead many astray. Yet He had given this warning only to add: 'But do not be alarmed; these things must happen, but the end is not yet. . . . The good news of the Kingdom will be proclaimed throughout the whole world as a witness to all nations; and then the end will come.'[1] When the years of grace were inaugurated, their charter was given in terms of this same expanding prospect: 'You will receive power when the Holy Spirit has come upon you; and you will be my witnesses in Jerusalem and in all Judaea, and in Samaria, and to the end of the earth.'[2] So began the Acts of the Apostles. 'For', writes Dr. Cullmann, 'the conviction is common to the whole of early Christianity that the end can only come after the Gospel has been offered to all nations.'[3] Undoubtedly the traditional Christian thought

---

[1] Matt. xxiv. 6–14 and Mark xiii. 7–13.
[2] Acts i. 8.
[3] *Christus und die Zeit*, p. 63 n.

of later ages did much less than justice to the grandeur and promise of this expanding prospect—that 'triumphal progress in Christ', as St. Paul calls it, in which 'the fragrance of the knowledge of God is diffused through us in every place'.[1] And the modern belief in progress, however fatally it may have deflected and detached itself from the wholeness of that Christian outlook to which it owes its original inspiration and, in so doing, fallen victim to intemperate excesses for which we are now paying a heavy price, must be admitted to have played some part in recalling us to this element of our Christian heritage. Just as we cannot fail to detect behind the missionary zeal of St. Paul a confidence in the future differently tempered from anything we find in the ages of tradition, so it is no accident that the greatest period in the later history of missionary expansion was also the period in which men looked forward to the earthly future with most confident hope.

It cannot reasonably be denied that the expectation of a blessed consummation lying beyond the end of earthly history takes on an air of unreality when the possible term of that history is extended from a few decades to a future of unimaginable length. It is not altogether easy to entertain a lively hope for something that is quite likely not to happen during the next ten million years. Hence it was natural that New Testament symbols such as the Second Advent, the Last Judgement and the General Resurrection should have become less determinative of the Christian consciousness as the envisaged period of earthly history

[1] 2 Cor. ii. 14.

was more and more extended; and it was perhaps natural also that the interest originally taken in them should in considerable part be transferred to the destiny immediately awaiting those who meanwhile die—that is, transferred from the race's journey along the platform to the individual's journey across it. Nevertheless, when such transference of interest is allowed to go too far, the whole Christian outlook on history is seriously endangered. It may therefore justly be claimed that the modern belief in earthly progress, however great its weaknesses, was nearer to New Testament thought than that (roughly contemporaneous) type of Christian eschatology which was content to exhaust itself in the contemplation of the immortality of the soul to the neglect of any teaching about the end of history; and in proportion as we ourselves have to admit that the concept of the end has relaxed its hold upon our thoughts and imaginations through envisagement of its immensely increased possible remoteness, we must hold all the more firmly to such belief in progress as we have, in the foregoing pages, found ourselves able and indeed obliged to retain. On the other hand, if we should allow ourselves to rest content with this intra-historical hope, banishing from our minds all Christian symbols of the end, all the old errors of secular progressivism must swiftly return to destroy us. The true purpose of these symbols is to serve as limiting conceptions, and as such they must certainly be retained. It is only when they are conceived as dateable events of a kind similar to the events of history itself—only when the end of time and space is regarded as from within time and space and given, as it were, a temporal dating and a spatial location—that the Second Advent, the Last Judgement and the General Resurrection fail in their effective grasp upon our thought and life. But when taken as symbols of a reality unimaginable by us save in this symbolic form, they become quite indispensable, protecting us against complacent satisfaction with an earthly order in which we are at best 'strangers and pilgrims', without robbing that order of all significance through the concentration of interest on an event conceived as lying in the distant future.[1]

We must now, however, raise the further question whether the Christian should envisage the progressive evangelization of the nations merely as an open possibility or is entitled to regard it as certainly promised to him by the principles of his faith. This question is discussed in a striking article, entitled 'Victory in This World', con-

---

[1] Cf. Reinhold Niebuhr, *The Nature and Destiny of Man* (1943), Vol. II, pp. 299–301. 'The symbol of the second coming of Christ can neither be taken literally nor dismissed as unimportant. . . . If the symbol is taken literally, the dialectical conception of time and eternity is falsified and the ultimate vindication of God over history is reduced to a point in history. . . . On the other hand if the symbol is dismissed as unimportant . . . the Biblical dialectic is obscured in another direction. All theologies which do not take these symbols seriously will be discovered on close analysis not to take history seriously either. They presuppose an eternity which annuls rather than fulfils the historical process. . . . Against utopianism the Christian faith insists that the final consummation of history lies beyond the conditions of the temporal process. Against other-worldliness it asserts that the consummation fulfils, rather than negates, the historical process. There is no way of expressing this dialectical concept without running the danger of its dissolution. The dissolution has, in fact, taken place again and again in Christian history. Those who believed in the simple fulfilment of history have been arrayed against those who believed that historical existence was robbed of its meaning in the final consummation. Both parties to the debate used Christian symbols to express their half-Christian convictions.'

tributed to the *International Review of Missions* by the late
Principal David Cairns in April 1942. Cairns is here concerned to defend the certain assurance of victory against
the contrary view that human history will be 'a ding-
dong battle all the way with the good becoming better
and the bad worse till the end comes'.[1] He proceeds by
way of a careful analysis of the teaching of the missionary
hymns included in a typical modern hymn-book, and
he finds that two-thirds of these are 'prayers of expectant
hope', while the remainder are confident assurances of the
world's conversion. Two of the latter may here be quoted
as examples. One is Isaac Watts's familiar early eighteenth-
century hymn which begins:

> Jesus shall reign where'er the sun
> Does his successive journeys run,
> His Kingdom stretch from shore to shore
> Till moons shall wax and wane no more.

'Nothing', adds Cairns, 'could be more explicit than that
in its assertion of the victory of the Gospel in earth, space
and time.' The other is the eighteenth-century Scottish
paraphrase, 'Behold! the mountain of the Lord':

> The beam that shines from Zion hill
> Shall lighten every land;
> The King who reigns in Salem's towers
> Shall all the world command . . .
>
> No strife shall rage, nor hostile feuds
> Disturb those peaceful years;
> To ploughshares men shall beat their swords,
> To pruning-hooks their spears.

[1] Cairns apparently takes the phrase 'a ding-dong battle' from C. H.
Dodd, *History and the Gospel*, p. 169.

No longer hosts encountering hosts
Shall crowds of slain deplore:
They hang their trumpet in the hall,
And study war no more.

It is significant to find such a writer as Professor Macmurray coming to what appears to be the same conclusion, namely, that the triumph of Christianity in history must be regarded by Christians as certain.

'Since action is the realization of intention, to think of history as the action of God is to think of it as the realization of the intention of God. Since God is Absolute, it is nonsensical to think that His intention in history will not be realized. For this reason any statement of what the intention of God is in history is also a statement of *what will in fact be realized* in the future. Thus the spiritual understanding of the will of God for man (which is what we represent as an "ethic") is *ipso facto* an understanding of what will happen to man in the future—our "apocalyptic".'[1]

And his book concludes with the words:

'The fundamental law of human nature cannot be broken. "He that saveth his life will lose it." The will to power is self-frustrating. It is the meek who will inherit the earth.'[2]

There is no doubt that the New Testament lends strong support to such a reading. What we find there is no mere exhortation, in the imperative, to spread the Gospel to the ends of the earth, but also the indicative statement that it will be so spread: 'grace becoming greater through the greater number of those to whom it extends'.[3] St. Mark's 'The good news must first be proclaimed to all nations' becomes in St. Matthew, 'This good news of the King-

---

[1] *The Clue to History*, p. 93 f.
[2] Ibid., p. 237.
[3] 2 Cor. iv. 15: ἡ χάρις πλεονάσασα διὰ τῶν πλειόνων.

dom will be proclaimed throughout the whole world.' The injunction 'Go therefore and make disciples of all nations' is accompanied by the promise, 'Lo, I am with you always, to the close of the age'.[1] The promise before Pentecost was 'You will be (ἔσεσθε) My witnesses . . . to the end of the earth.' Dr. Cullmann rightly points out that what such passages affirm is not that all men will be converted but only that the good news will be proclaimed to all; but he places so much weight on this distinction as to impart a certain unreality and artificiality to the promise. 'It is not', he writes, 'as if the coming of the Kingdom were dependent on the *success* of the proclamation; it is dependent only on the *fact* of its having been made.'[2] But to draw the line so cleanly at this point is to cramp the faith of St. Paul, who seems to have confidently believed also in the success of the proclamation.

'A callousness has come over part of Israel until the plenitude of the Gentiles shall come in, and so all Israel will be saved. . . . For God has consigned all to disobedience, that He may have mercy on all.'[3]

'He has made known to us in all wisdom and understanding the mystery of His will, according to His purpose which He set forth in Christ, as a plan for the fullness of the times, to bring all things in heaven and earth to a head in Christ.'[4]

'In Him the whole [divine] fullness was pleased to dwell, and through Him to reconcile all things, alike on earth and in heaven, to Himself, making peace by the blood of His cross.'[5]

'He must reign until He has put all things under His feet.'[6]

We have indeed no warrant for understanding St.

---

[1] Matt. xxviii. 18–20.   [2] *Christus und die Zeit*, p. 141.
[3] Rom. xi. 25, 32.   [4] Eph. i. 9–10.
[5] Col. i. 19 f.   [6] 1 Cor. xv. 25.

Paul to mean that a time will ever come when every living individual will have accepted the Gospel. If Dr. Cullmann had said no more than this, we should have had to agree: for in these passages (as so often) the Apostle is thinking, not in terms of individuals, but in terms of nations and historical movements. But the fact remains that with the full assurance of faith he forecasts the world-wide success of the Christian mission within the time still remaining to it; and, as Dr. Dodd justly remarks in his commentary on the first of the above-quoted passages, 'He may be allowed to have meant what he said in its full sense.'[1] No doubt the difficulty we feel about such an act of faith, our hesitation about turning a hopeful possibility into an assured forecast, is part of the much more general difficulty we have in resolving the antinomy of grace and free will. And we may suspect that in resting his case upon the premise 'since God is Absolute', Professor Macmurray yields too much to the predestinarian side of the argument and too little to the libertarian. Nevertheless, when the large-scale movement of history has been in question, the classical Christian tradition has never hesitated to give the precedence to a providential dispensation of things that overrules all human disobedience for the fulfilment of a gracious eternal purpose. In the course of our study we have had frequent occasion to mark the uncertainty with which modern champions of progress have faced the question whether the realization of such progress is inevitable or only an open possibility. We must accord them some

---

[1] *The Epistle to the Romans* (Moffatt New Testament Commentary), 1932, p. 185 f.

sympathy, because the exigency in which they find themselves is only a secularized form of an exigency to which
we must all confess. On the other hand, we are at liberty
to point out that in being thus secularized, the genuinely
antinomic character of the issue is degraded to that of a
choice between quite intractable contradictories, because
both the freedom and the determination must now be conceived as immanent in the historical process itself, and
therefore as standing on a single level of relevance.

§ 35

Our conclusion then is that the Christian faith does offer
us a very confident hope for the future course of terrestrial history. It is a hope which has been too little represented in the Christian tradition, but to which we are now
recalled. We must recover that sense of standing on the
threshold of a new historical economy (or dispensation),
that sense of a noble prospect opening out before us, that
sense of the power of the Spirit and of the inexhaustible
resources now available to us, that adventurous zeal for
the renewal of humanity and that confidence in ultimate
victory of which the New Testament is so full. We must
allow that one cause of the emergence of the secularized
and distorted version of the Christian hope which it has
been our present concern to study and to refute, has been
the felt need of compensating for the apparent defeatism
that characterized so much of traditional Christian
thought. What we have, however, sought to do in this
final chapter, is to redress the balance in a way that is at

once more consonant with original Christianity and less vulnerable to legitimate and fair-minded attack.

But now the votaries of progress are likely to exclaim, 'What is this alternative that you offer us? It is a hope for the success of an evangelistic campaign and above all, it would seem, for the progressive success of Foreign Missions!' And the stridency of the exclamation will reveal that there are no two projects in the world in which they conceive themselves to be less interested.

Such an objection can be met only by a further reminder of how the evangelic and missionary task was conceived by the first generation of Christians. Evangel is the Greek word for good news, and what the first Christian evangelists and missionaries were concerned to do was to communicate to all men, even to the farthest corners of the earth, what they were convinced was the best piece of news that had ever fallen upon human ears. This news was to the effect that by the gracious providence of God a new era had now dawned in human history which gave promise of complete renewal. 'If any man be in Christ, there is a new creation; old things are bygone, and lo, new things are coming into being.'[1] Our current system of dating all events forwards or backwards from Christ's advent symbolizes at once the wide welcome which soon came to be given to this good news and the realistic way in which its portent was understood. Its acceptance came, in fact, to provide the ultimate differentiating character of the culture of the modern West.

It is of this Western culture that the modern apostles

[1] 2 Cor. v, 17.

of progress are the children, and therefore it is not surprising that they too should profess a hope of world renewal. They too have good news to announce, and they too are anxious to carry it to all nations, even to earth's remotest bound—and indeed have achieved no mean success in doing so. They too, therefore, are evangelists and missionaries in their own kind. Moreover, many of them are not so entirely out of sympathy with the original foundations of our culture as to deny that the year one of our era did really mark a significant watershed in history and the opening out of something like a new prospect for humanity. These would, therefore, be by no means in opposition to any endeavours that are made to spread what are acknowledgedly Christian principles of conduct, Christian norms of individual and community life, throughout the whole of human society. But they desire this to be done within the intellectual cabinet, not of the original Christian outlook, but of that alternative cosmic outlook of their own, the stability of whose foundations we have found so much reason to call in question.

As against such counsellors the Christian missionary enterprise stands only for the conviction that no part of the great hope which the preaching of the good news brought long ago to that old and out-worn Mediterranean world, and later on to the men of our Northern races, can continue to maintain itself in disseverance from the wholeness of its original context. It is therefore not interested in the propagation among men of other races of a kind of vaguely 'Christianized' culture, which in practice means only a secularized Western culture calculated to destroy the indigenous spirituality, such as it is, without offering any substantial spiritual substitute.[1] On the other hand the Christian mission can justify its own disturbance, sometimes amounting to complete destruction, of the indigenous cultures (a disturbance or destruction which is inevitable in view of the close integration of general culture with the existing religion in the immense majority of pagan lands), if it understands and does its best to communicate the full significance of the Christian Gospel as proclaiming not only a message of individual salvation, and not only an apocalyptic promise of final salvation beyond the frontier of death or after the end of history, but also a message of the present and progressive renewal of communal and social life in all its aspects and departments. When the Christian missionary task is so understood, we can commend it to our progressivist contemporaries with all boldness, and without any fear of its appearing as a contemptible substitute for the differently tempered hopes of which they are so loath to divest themselves. Far from offering them a stone in place of the bread our argument has attempted to deny them, we are offering them rather that better bread, the Bread of Life, whereof whoso eats shall not hunger again.

While, as we have seen, the underlying principles of

[1] Cf. Arnold J. Toynbee, *Civilization on Trial* (1948), p. 84 f.: 'For some two hundred years, dating from the beginning of the da Gaman era, our world-storming Western forefathers made a valiant attempt to propagate abroad the whole of our Western cultural heritage, including its religious core as well as its technological rind; and in this they were surely well-inspired; for every culture is a "whole" whose parts are subtly inter-dependent, and to export the husk without the grain may be as deadly as to radiate the satellite electrons of an atom without the nucleus.'

apostolic thought fully warrant this larger conception of the evangelic mission, more specific guidance is often lacking. The apostles have not a little to say about the proper behaviour of a tiny Christian minority set in the midst of an immense and powerful pagan society, and about the proper attitude of Christian men towards the rulers of such a society. But in the nature of the case they could have nothing specific to say about the Christian direction of society as a whole or about the behaviour of a Christian man who is himself a ruler. Yet those of us who live in states having any claim to be called democratic are all rulers; democracy being but the Greek word for rule by the people. As St. Paul looked forward into the short expanse of terrestrial history which he supposed to lie ahead, he believed himself charged to carry the transforming and recreative message of the Gospel to all the nations of that *orbis terrarum*, that 'circle of the lands', which alone was known to him; but there is no sign that his thought carried forward to the point of asking how the general culture of those lands should be adjusted, and their general society conducted, if and when Christians should ever find themselves beginning to have a voice in such matters. For us, however, such questions are inevitable. Christians have now had large influence, and over large areas the controlling influence, in the moulding of general culture for a period immensely longer than St. Paul supposed to be available for the entire missionary task, and it is their prayer that such influence may be further extended during such years of grace as are still granted them. Hence when the Church of to-day looks forward through the years, its vision of progress is not only of an increase in the number of Christian individuals but of the increasing Christianization of the whole life of the community.

Such a Christian influence on general culture has now been with us for some fifteen hundred years. During that period the organization of society, the laws of nations, the education of youth, the development of all the arts, musical, dramatic, architectural, plastic, pictorial and the rest, together with many other things, have been, to say the least, profoundly affected by the impact of the Christian mission. Recent thought has been particularly concerned to point out that even the advance of modern empirical science is a result of the Christian mission, in spite of the difficulty the Church has had in coming to terms with its later developments—a difficulty which may derive as much from the scientists' misunderstanding of the limits of their own competence as from the Church's failure to rise to the fullness of the Gospel entrusted to it. Professor Macmurray indeed goes so far as to claim that science is not only 'the product of Christianity' but 'its most adequate expression so far'.[1] But we can set aside this last judgement as extreme without invalidating the contention much more generally represented, that modern natural science was first rendered possible when the pagan subjection of man to a nature controlled by demonic powers was replaced by the Christian conviction (so central to the whole New Testament consciousness of the dawn of a new age) that these powers had now been de-

[1] *The Clue to History*, p. 86. Cf. also p. 192.

cisively subdued. 'The greatest contribution of Christianity,' Berdyaev writes, 'although it is not fully recognized by the Christian world, consisted in that it liberated man from the power of the baser elemental nature and demons.' The mechanization of nature is one of the 'secondary results' of this.

'However paradoxical it may seem, I am convinced that Christianity alone made possible both positive science and technique. As long as man had found himself in communion with nature and had based his life upon mythology, he could not raise himself above nature through an act of apprehension by means of the natural sciences or technique. It is impossible for man to build railways, invent the telegraph or telephone, while living in the fear of demons. Thus for man to be able to treat nature like a mechanism, it is necessary for the demonic inspiration of nature and man's communion with it to have died out in the human consciousness. The mechanical conception of the world was to lead to a revolt against Christianity, but it was itself the spiritual result of liberating man from elemental nature and its demons.'[1]

Yet while the reality of the Christian culture of past ages is in no way to be denied or the measure of its achievements to be despised, the present state of our so-called Christian civilization forces us to realize how slowly and how faultily, with what fitful obedience to the heavenly vision, and with lapses how frequent into apostasy, we have advanced on the road that lay open before us. The Church's first duty is therefore to repent her grievous failure of stewardship, abasing herself before the Lord

[1] *The Meaning of History* (English translation), pp. 113–17. Cf. also a notable article by Michael Foster in *The Christian News-Letter*, No. 299, 26th November 1947; A. D. Ritchie, *Civilization, Science and Religion*, pp. 168 ff.; Charles E. Raven, *Religion and Science: A Diagnosis* (1946).

whose cause she has so greatly hindered, but also humbling herself before a world whose true weal she has so defectively served. True repentance, however, must be a repentance unto life and a resolve to further endeavour; so that it is likewise the Church's duty to pray for an enlarged vision of a world in which Christ reigns as King, and to go forward with increased hopefulness to the ever-widening tasks and opportunities which such a vision entails. To revert to only one of our examples, but to choose that one which might be regarded as most extreme: it is a true part of the mission of Christian evangelism to seek to compose the misunderstanding at present existing between our scientific and our religious thinking. And this is a task the successful accomplishment of which can by no means be ensured by the conversion of more individual scientists to a full Christian commitment, eagerly as that is to be desired. For since the division is not between scientists and Christians but is, as often as not, within the Christian mind itself, it can be overcome only by an arduous labour of Christian philosophy.

There is, however, one misconstruction against which, in view of the confusion caused in our minds by the modern versions of progress, it may still be necessary to guard ourselves. The advance for which we are encouraged to hope, as the years of grace flow on, is not the emergence of a more consecrated type of Christian character than past ages have to show us. There is in this respect no carry-over from generation to generation, but every individual must make a new beginning for himself. It is only insight and understanding that are cumulative, and while this means that a new generation of men is likely to be confronted with new and, in a sense, more advanced alternatives than were presented to the old, it does not mean that the former is any more likely than the latter to act according to knowledge. This point was clearly made, in criticism of prevailing progressivist ideas, by the German theologian Martin Kähler in a remarkable essay written as early as 1865. The progress of mankind, he argued, is a reality in the sense of 'a gradual Christianizing of the nations and a closer approximation to the moral ideal of public life', yet 'it remains unalterably true that every individual, by right of that very freedom wherein his dignity resides, begins a new history in his own personal moral growth'.[1] Such a reminder delivers us at one stroke from many absurdities, including the insufferably arrogant absurdity of supposing that the saints of long ago yesterdays must have been less saintly than those of to-day or to-morrow. What may legitimately be hoped for, as the pattern of the years of grace unfolds itself, is not the appearance of a better race of men, but a wider and fuller understanding of the tasks to which Christian men must devote themselves; not a more scrupulous conscientiousness but an enlarged and better instructed conscience.

A careful discrimination of this kind was already made by T. H. Green in his comparison of the Hellenic with the Christian ideal. 'The will to be good', he claimed, 'is not

---

[1] *Der Menschheit Fortschritt und des Menschen Ewigkeit.* The writer's attention was directed to this essay by his friend and former student, the Rev. John Moffat, now of Rajputana.

purer or stronger in him [the Christian] than it must have been in any Greek who came near to the philosopher's ideal, but the recognition of new social claims compels its exercise in a new and larger self-denial.' Therefore, 'we give the advantage to the Christian type because it implies, directly on the part of those by whom it is exhibited, and indirectly on the part of the multitude by whose claims it is elicited, a liberation of their powers unknown to the ancient world'.[1] Yet though we have been arguing for the application of this kind of distinction to the comparison of the Christian saints of earlier ages with the most devoted Christian spirits of our own day, we cannot agree that it can be so simply applied to the comparison of Christian saints with Greek sages. In the former comparison we have to do with the same motivation throughout, but in the latter account has to be taken of a profound difference of motive such as sets the whole spiritual scene, as well as the whole of moral endeavour, in a new perspective. Green is right in saying that many a pagan was as conscientiously devoted to his ideals as have been the Christian saints to theirs; and there are many parallel instances of this in the Indian and Mohammedan worlds of to-day. But the difference is not merely in 'the recognition of new social claims'. The very devotion itself is differently tempered.

In saying this last we are pointing to what is the most serious curtailment of the modern belief in progress which

---

[1] *Prolegomena to Ethics*, §§ 271, 278. In his early book on *Moral Order and Progress* (1889) Samuel Alexander follows Green closely; see pp. 282, 389, etc. Cf. also Arnold J. Toynbee, *Civilization on Trial* (1948), pp. 248, 261–2.

our study has forced upon us. We have found little reason
to believe in a general line of spiritual advance running
through the various spiritual traditions and from one tradition to another—little reason to believe that in this
innermost sphere 'the thoughts of men are widen'd by
the process of the suns'.[1] The hope we have been able to
defend is rather of the progressive expansion of a single
tradition, namely, the Christian. For such a curtailment
we can, however, claim the support of a number of recent
investigators, by no means all of whom have approached
the question from the point of view of Christian faith,
and especially of those belonging to the sociological
school roughly associated with the names of Alfred
Weber, Max Weber and Ernst Troeltsch. These have
contended that spiritual insight does not follow a single
rectilinear course through human history but rather radiates from a number of quite separate centres. Just as it has
been said that 'there is no such thing in the world as
religion, there are only religions', so these now say that
there is no such thing as general progress but only the
progressive enrichment of disparate spiritual traditions.
There is, of course, a highest common factor that may
be extracted from the different religions, consisting of
certain mental dispositions, ideas and practices reappear-
ing in them all; but this common factor could not possibly, in isolation from one or other of its rich natural
contexts, possess a vitality of its own such as to bring
about any development in its own right. As Hegel
somewhere says in a figure, 'you cannot eat fruit in

[1] Tennyson, 'Locksley Hall'.

general, but only particular fruits like plums, pears, apricots'.

It will be remembered that at the beginning of our study we were led to make a distinction between the technical and the broadly spiritual aspects of culture and at the same time to recognize that certain cultural phenomena seem, in words we quoted from Dr. Marett, 'to face both ways at once', manifesting both a technical and also a spiritual aspect. Reference may now usefully be made to the somewhat different analysis offered by Alfred Weber in recognition of these same facts. He sharply distinguishes, not two, but three quite independent lines of historical development—the social process, the process of civilization, and the succession of cultures. A single pattern of social process can be traced in all societies, manifesting in spite of all variations the same typical stages in each; this being the evolution of what he calls society's bodily (*körperhaft*) existence. By the process of civilization, on the other hand, he means the advancing intellectual or rational understanding of the world. This follows a logical development, and reaches conclusions that are universally valid and can be carried without difficulty across all social and cultural boundaries from one tradition to another; it forms an intermediate territory (*Zwischenreich*) which in different ways serves the social process (by providing it with improved practical techniques) and the realm of spiritual culture (by providing it with improved intellectual instruments). The movement of culture itself is, however, of an entirely different kind from the other two processes and is governed by quite

other laws, its business being to satisfy the needs of the
'soul' of society as distinct from its 'body'. It produces no
objective intellectual system, but rather 'a spiritually adjusted system of symbols' (*ein seelisch bedingtes Nebeneinan-
der von Symbolen*).

'This sphere does not create a cosmos of universally valid and
necessary things; for all that here emerges is and remains enclosed
by its very nature within the historical traditions in which it origin-
ates and with which it is inwardly bound up. . . . In the cultural
movement of the various historical traditions we are in fact presented with the formation of entirely separate "worlds", which
arise and perish along with these traditions, are individually as unique
as they are mutually exclusive, and are all totally different in nature
from the common cosmos fashioned by the process of civilization.'

'The view taken of the movement of culture by the evolutionary
philosophy of history has its origin in the confusion of the intellectual
with the spiritual (*seelisch*) sphere under the inclusive concept of
"mind" (*Geist*), and in the consequent subsumption of the process
of civilization and the movement of culture under the single inclusive idea of "mental development" (*geistige Entwicklung*); an amal-
gam for which the eighteenth century prepared the way and which
German idealism brought to completion.'[1]

It is not necessary to accept Weber's threefold scheme
in its entirety, or to adopt his German usage of the terms
'culture' and 'civilization', in order to follow him in his
main conclusion, namely, that history reveals a number
of essentially disparate spiritual traditions, each with its
own characteristic and untransplantable religious outlook,
moral code, and taste and style in art. Nor again is it
necessary to follow him in the quaint and perverse con-

[1] 'Prinzipielles zur Kultursoziologie' in *Archiv für Sozialwissenschaft und
Sozialpolitik*, Band 47, 1920–21, pp. 1–49.

tention (represented also in a milder form by Troeltsch) that when the so-called universal religions of Christianity, Islam and Buddhism have been transplanted to new social settings they have become entirely different religions— the Hinayana Buddhism of Ceylon being a different religion from the Mahayana of the Far East, and the various Christian sects of later times being religions as separate from one another as they all are from primitive Christianity. This is carrying a true insight to an absurd and pedantic extreme. The great missionary religions are no whit less entitled than are systems like Hinduism and Confucianism to be regarded as ultimate and irreducible units in the spiritual history of our race.

Moreover, it is the religious systems rather than the successive civilizations that must be accorded this status. The former rather than the latter are the historical wholes (or *Geschichtskörper*, as Weber calls them) within which any spiritual progress is to be looked for. This is the view defended by Dr. Toynbee, who argues that instead of religion being subsidiary to the reproduction of secular civilizations, the successive rises and falls of such civilizations are subsidiary to the growth of religion—'stepping-stones to higher things on the religious plane'. Each civilization may exhibit the same familiar cycle of birth, youth, maturity, decay and final disintegration, so that the succession of such civilizations does not provide history as a whole with any general direction; that can only be provided by a religious impulse which carries over from one civilization to another. In a fine figure:

'If religion is a chariot, it looks as if the wheels on which it mounts towards Heaven may be the periodic downfalls of civilizations on Earth. It looks as if the movement of civilizations may be cyclic and recurrent, while the movement of religion may be on a single continuous upward line. The continuous upward movement of religion may be served and promoted by the cyclic movement of civilizations round the cycle of birth, death, birth.'[1]

The part of this thesis which suggests that the perishing of civilizations has a positive part to play in aiding spiritual advance need not here concern us, the point we are anxious to establish being only that religious systems are the real centres from which spiritual (as distinct from merely technical) progress must, if it occurs at all, be expected to radiate.

But has progress in fact radiated from the pagan centres of spirituality, that is, from those religious systems which have themselves possessed no idea of progress, nor any historical outlook over future time, such as characterizes Biblical religion alone? If progress is to mean what we have understood it to mean throughout our enquiry, namely, movement in a desirable direction, this does not follow. Some of these systems undoubtedly display a certain 'development', their latent genius requiring some considerable time in which to manifest itself fully. We may speak, for instance, of a Hindu view of life which better understands its own nature in the Brahmanas than in the Rig Veda, and in the Upanishads than in the Brahmanas; and under the inspiration of this advancing insight there was a gradual flowering of Indian art. There

---

[1] *Civilization on Trial*, p. 235 f. Cf. *A Study of History*, Vol. IV, at the beginning; and Somervell's abridgement, p. 253—'a major irreversible movement which is borne on the wings of a minor repetitive movement'.

is thus a continuity of development within individual systems which cannot be traced through the succession of systems; and not a single development of art running through all the ages of mankind but only a number of separate developments, each enclosed within its own total spiritual organism. On the other hand, it is only from the point of view of the characteristic spiritual impulse originally inspiring it that any one of these developments can, without further examination, be regarded as marking an advance. It may be a genuine enrichment of the particular tradition, yet may appear to the adherents of other traditions as a change, not for the better, but for the worse, implying only the increasingly inpenitent induration of an original error. At all events, the further progress for which Christians may hope can only be that which radiates from the Christian centre of history, and can be nothing else than the progressive embodiment in the life of humanity of the mind that was in Christ and 'a growing up in all things unto Him who is the Head'.[1]

[1] Eph. iv. 15.

INDEX